What others are saying about *Amazed by Grace!*

Amazed by Grace *is a reassuring tour through the garden of God's touchpoints with His children. Cindy has lined the path with many names of faith, each one confirming again the veracity of Jeremiah's cry in the dark: "Great is Thy faithfulness!" Digest this book to validate your own faith in the God of grace.*

Jeanne Hendricks, author, *Women of Honor*

Amazed by Grace *is well titled. Here is a handbook for the reader who wants to go deeper in his or her spiritual walk. Not only is this a helpful resource book for leaders, but it is also the amazing story of Cindy's life. I read it with great personal interest and enrichment.*

Ingrid Trobisch, founder, Family Life Mission, and author, *The Confident Woman*

For anyone wounded in life by a lack of grace freely extended when needed the most, Cindy McDowell's reminders of God's eternal grace are healing words for a troubled soul. Intermingling her own grace stories with a plethora of additional resources, she traces the pathway to authentic grace. With her own unique wit and joyful elegance, Cindy captures you from the opening pages of Amazed by Grace *and carries you through this subject like a stretcher bearer. The topic of grace is given fine treatment through the weaving together of poignant Scripture, life application questions, memory verses, several hymns, and lots of helpful stories. Thanks, Cindy, for this gift of love to all who need reminders that His grace is sufficient for each new day!*

Stephen A. Macchia, president,
Evangelistic Association of New England

Amazed by Grace *is rightly titled, for grace runs throughout this helpful and inspiring book by Lucinda Secrest McDowell. God's grace breaks through again and again in delightful and refreshing ways. Read Cindy's excellent book and drench yourself in God's liberating grace!*

Donald W. Morgan, author,
How to Get It Together When Your World Is Coming Apart

She lives it! Others show their best sides; Cindy tells it like it is. Amazed by Grace *presents tender and tough experiences of grace from a God who is there.*

Miriam Adeney, senior editor, *Christianity Today*

◆

Tired of trying to make sure
God is pleased with you? If you've
realized you can't do it on your own,
get ready to be

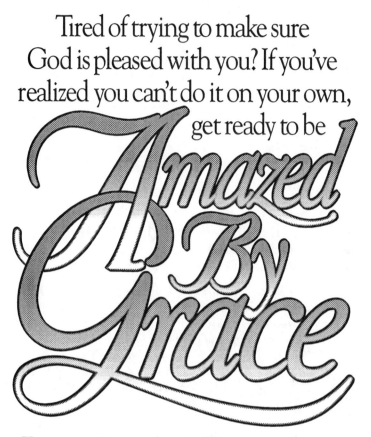

Amazed By Grace

LUCINDA SECREST
McDOWELL

FOREWORD BY GAIL MACDONALD

BROADMAN
& HOLMAN
PUBLISHERS

Nashville, Tennessee

Printed in the United States of America

Published by
Broadman & Holman Publishers
Nashville, Tennessee

Designed by
Steven Boyd

4261-84
0-8054-6184-1

Dewey Decimal Classification: 234.1
Subject Heading: GRACE (THEOLOGY) \ CHRISTIAN LIFE \
BURN OUT (PSYCHOLOGY)
Library of Congress Card Catalog Number: 95-23228

Unless otherwise noted, Scripture quotations are from the Holy Bible,
New International Version, © 1973, 1978, 1984 by International
Bible Society. Others are NRSV, New Revised Standard Version of the
Bible, © 1989 by the Division of Christian Education of the National
Council of Churches of Christ in the United States of America, used by
permission, all rights reserved; and The Message, the New Testament
in Contemporary English, © 1993 by Eugene H. Peterson, published
by NavPress, Colorado Springs, Colo.

Library of Congress Cataloging-in-Publication Data

McDowell, Lucinda Secrest, 1953–
    Amazed by grace / Lucinda Secrest McDowell.
      p.cm.
    Includes bibliographical references.
    ISBN 0-8054-6184-1
    1. Grace (Theology). 2. Christian life. I. Title.
BT761.2.M385 1996
234—dc20

95-23228
CIP

00 99 98 97 96 5 4 3 2 1

Tired of trying to make sure
God is pleased with you? If you've
realized you can't do it on your own,
get ready to be

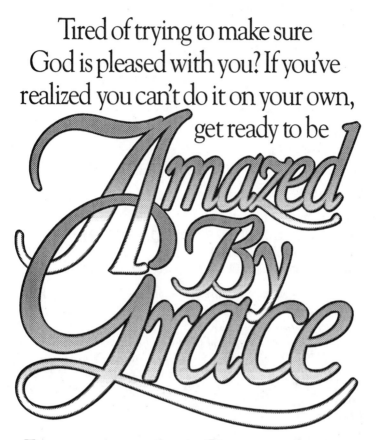

LUCINDA SECREST MCDOWELL

FOREWORD BY GAIL MACDONALD

BROADMAN
& HOLMAN
PUBLISHERS

Nashville, Tennessee

Printed in the United States of America

Published by
Broadman & Holman Publishers
Nashville, Tennessee

Designed by
Steven Boyd

4261-84
0-8054-6184-1

Dewey Decimal Classification: 234.1
Subject Heading: GRACE (THEOLOGY) \ CHRISTIAN LIFE \
BURN OUT (PSYCHOLOGY)
Library of Congress Card Catalog Number: 95-23228

Unless otherwise noted, Scripture quotations are from the Holy Bible,
New International Version, © 1973, 1978, 1984 by International
Bible Society. Others are NRSV, New Revised Standard Version of the
Bible, © 1989 by the Division of Christian Education of the National
Council of Churches of Christ in the United States of America, used by
permission, all rights reserved; and The Message, the New Testament
in Contemporary English, © 1993 by Eugene H. Peterson, published
by NavPress, Colorado Springs, Colo.

Library of Congress Cataloging-in-Publication Data

McDowell, Lucinda Secrest, 1953–
    Amazed by grace / Lucinda Secrest McDowell.
    p.cm.
    Includes bibliographical references.
    ISBN 0-8054-6184-1
    1. Grace (Theology). 2. Christian life. I. Title.
BT761.2.M385 1996
234—dc20

95-23228
CIP

00 99 98 97 96 5 4 3 2 1

For my children
Justin Thomas Gregory McDowell
Timothy Michael Laurens McDowell
Fiona Johanna Yvonne McDowell
Margaret Sarah Secrest McDowell
and my husband
Thomas Michael McDowell

"Thanks for the grace!"
◆

Contents

◆

Foreword

_____

_T_ _here are no super-Christians, only super-receivers._ I don't remember who gave me the gift of those words, but they came at a time in my life when I needed them. Grace is something we receive because we have realized our broken condition before God. How many times I have heard my husband, Gordon, say, "If Christians could only discover the power of repentance, our churches would never be the same."

How so? Isn't it because repentance unleashes the dynamic energy of grace? And that's what a cross-focused life is all about. Surely the enemy of our souls cringes whenever grace is understood and given, because he never received it.

Gordon and I have been the recipients of God's amazing grace, as well as the grace of many people, so we enjoy reading about how others have experienced grace. In the past ten years, we have heard hundreds of stories of how grace has been given or withheld. What a difference it makes when grace is given, instead of judgment! Not a cheap grace that overlooks evil, mind you, but a grace that stands beneath the cross, stares evil in the face, and says, "Evil, you will not win!"

I have always been encouraged to realize that James, Jesus' brother, said, "Mercy is greater than judgment" (James 2:13). Mercy ignites grace. If one who spent almost thirty years living in the same home with Jesus can come away with that understanding, then anything I learn about God's kindness or grace will certainly help me grow in Christlikeness.

In *Amazed by Grace* Cindy Secrest McDowell has given us many moving pictures of how grace has made the amazing difference in her life as well as in the multitude of her "book friends," both living and dead.

My earliest recollections of Cindy come from her single years. Even as a younger woman, she insisted that each experience and reading be pressed into growth. She read widely, not only from Scripture and current authors, but from the classics that often were eschewed by young people now and then. I found myself looking forward to Cindy's Christmas greetings, because I knew they would be well thought out and have an idea or quote that would be substantial and challenging.

It is this life attitude—to make everything serve—that makes it possible for Cindy to write such a challenging book. It's full of substance derived from years of asking questions, observing people, and saying yes to afflictions that cause the grace life to flourish.

When she and Mike married, I knew she would adapt to the rigors of becoming a sacrificial and loving wife and mom. She has helped Mike, Justin, Timothy, Fiona, and

Maggie believe that if connected with the power of God, they can accomplish unbelievable things! Cindy has also given this gift of affirmation to the people at First Church of Christ in Wethersfield, too. I know. I have seen it firsthand.

As you read *Amazed by Grace*, I hope you will savor the many quotes and ideas in each chapter before moving on to the next. The Scriptures and questions at the end of each chapter encourage us to integrate what we have read into our daily living. Read on, enjoying a grace-filled life, even as Cindy reminds us of how she has!

Gail MacDonald
Lexington, Massachusetts

Acknowledgments

———

*P*eople are always asking me, "When do you write?" And I'm usually at a loss for a reasonable answer. I wish I could say that at specific times on certain days I chain myself to the computer and let the creative juices flow. I wish I could say that, but I can't. At this season of my life as a part-time minister, a full-time wife of a minister, and mother of four very active children ages six to twenty, my writing is important but not terribly scheduled.

The truth is I'm almost always "writing" in my mind. I once heard that "those who are writers can't not write." (Yes, I know that's a double negative, but it's a direct quote.) So, whether I'm observing life, studying the Bible, reading books, or participating in numerous activities which, on the surface, have nothing to do with writing, I'm always filtering experience through an artist's eyes. I write on slips of paper, dashboard notepads (yes, while I'm driving), checkbook deposit slips, the backs of PTO announcements, and even church bulletins (oops, don't tell). I fill notebooks with gleanings from my reading. I read all the time—much more than I write. And occasionally I'm privileged enough (or maybe desperate enough) to have twenty-four hours away to do the deep contemplative uninterrupted work of writing that can only come out of silence.

Another author friend, Sharon, who just finished her first book, sent me a quote by Catherine Marshall which seems very true: "You cannot be a writer unless you are willing to accept solitude. This means fewer meetings with friends, more nays than yeas to activities previously attended, and more quiet hours to develop inner horizons. Less TV and radio, less noise. More time to daydream, to study and pray, to read and think and dream. But especially more time to work, to research, outline, write and rewrite. . . ."

Actually, I have been "writing" this particular book my whole life, though it is only now that I have reduced it to words on paper. I'd like to thank the friends, acquaintances, and conference participants who inspired the following pages. Many of the names and locations have been disguised in this book, and some of the conversations are composites. I have included personal illustrations as I remember them (or as the scribbles in my years of journals remind me). *Amazed by Grace* could never have been completed without the help of many people, only a few of whom I am able to acknowledge here:

♦ My life's partner-in-grace, Michael McDowell, who helped me with perspective and filled in lots of gaps on the home front in order that I could meet my deadlines.

♦ My children—Justin, Tim, Fiona, and Maggie Sarah—who provided my inspiration, a few editorial deletions, and lots of understanding when I had to say, "Later. Mama's working on her book now!"

♦ My parents and lifelong encouragers, Pratt and Sarah Secrest, who sent me away (with my girls) to *Camp of the Woods* so I could be still by Lake Pleasant and "remember the stories."

♦ My editor at Broadman & Holman Publishers, Vicki Crumpton, a true professional and great friend who possesses that wonderful ability to discern potential in writers such as me and help us to bring it to fruition.

♦ Gail McDonald who graciously agreed to write the foreword in the middle of her busy life of writing, lecturing, counseling, teaching, and grandmothering.

♦ Friends Ed and Kay Zito who offered, among other things, the solitude and inspiration of a snowbound chalet in Quebec where many of these chapters were pounded out.

♦ Friends Ed and Faith Curtis who provided me with a computer since "nobody writes a book on a typewriter any more, Cindy!" And the many patient friends who helped usher me into "computer literacy."

♦ The women of my Evening Bible Study at First Church of Christ in Wethersfield, Connecticut, who prayed, wrote notes, and even sent me away to a lovely bed and breakfast for an intense time of research.

♦ Special writer friends—Marjorie Wallem Rowe, Mary Wilken, and Jane Benard—who pored through my rough manuscript and made excellent suggestions.

♦ Other author friends—Jeanne Zornes and Linda McGinn—who told me, "You can write this book!" So I did.

- ◆ Writing expert Sally Stuart who taught me such useful things as "query letters" in 1981 to "book contracts" in 1994.

- ◆ My favorite college professor, Dr. Albert Blackwell, perhaps the first one to impress upon me, through his life and words, that theological knowledge must be fleshed out in practical living.

- ◆ "Heartspring," my Christian Women's Speakers Circle, who pray for me and provide a *safe place.*

- ◆ All those who have touched my life in significant ways. Your actual name may or may not appear in this book, but you know who you are, and I thank you.

- ◆ My Lord and Savior Jesus Christ who daily grants me that which I don't deserve—*His grace!*

Lucinda Secrest McDowell
"Gracehaven"
Wethersfield, Connecticut
May 1995

◆

CHAPTER ONE

Amazed by Grace

a·'mazed vb: overwhelmed with wonder

*H*is name was Tom. Growing up in West Virginia, his best friend throughout childhood was Jack. Tom and Jack shared adventures and dreams. After graduation, both joined the service and were eventually sent to combat in Desert Storm.

Though their families didn't know each other well, both having sons overseas gave them a bond. And both were quite relieved when Tom and Jack returned safely home to begin college studies.

Shortly after this homecoming, one gray day in December, Jack visited Tom at home. During their time in Tom's room, a gunshot rang out. No one is quite sure what happened—but Tom was dead and Jack was alive.

Tom's parents, Mark and Lou, were understandably heartbroken. Jack and his folks were also shattered. What's a parent to do in such a situation? Mark and Lou, both followers of Christ, chose not to press charges against Jack or even subject him to an investigation. They felt his private grief over the death of his best friend was already more than he could bear. Instead, Tom's parents reached out to comfort Jack and his family.

Lou even invited Jack's mom, Mary, to her church's women's retreat, paying the way of Mary and her best friend. Two weeks after the shooting, both ladies were sitting in an audience listening to the Saturday evening presentation on grace. Their presence was a far more vivid embodiment of grace than any words of the guest speaker. How do I know? I was the out-of-town speaker for that weekend conference, led by God to teach on Galatians.

I have always found it difficult to define *grace* because, quite frankly, it doesn't make any sense. But in preparing for the conference I had run across some words from Chuck Swindoll that seemed appropriate:

> Let's imagine you have a six-year-old son whom you love dearly. Tragically, one day you discover that your son was horribly murdered. After a lengthy search the investigators of the crime find the killer. You have a choice. If you used every means in your power to kill the murderer for his crime, that would be *vengeance*. If, however, you're content to sit back and let the legal authorities take over and execute on him what is proper—a fair trial, a plea of guilty, capital punishment—that is *justice*. But if you should plea for the pardon of the murderer, forgive him completely, invite him into your home, and adopt him as your own son, that is *grace*.[1]

When I innocently shared this illustration at the conference I wondered what *I* would do if someone killed one of my own four children. Was it really possible to live out grace in such a way? My question was most certainly (and very surprisingly) answered that night in the presence of Lou and Mary. Actually, neither of them was able to make it through my whole talk, but the sharing and crying between them in the lounge was much more significant than my words to the two hundred others in the ballroom.

My choice of grace illustrations was not an accident—God had a divine appointment with all of us that weekend. He taught us more than we ever bargained for about grace.

Are *you* amazed by grace? Does the grace of God overwhelm you with wonder? Or are you baffled like the little girl in the cartoon who looks up at her minister and says, "Who's this 'Amazing Grace' you keep talking about?"

Lewis Smedes says,

> Grace is amazing because it works against the grain of common sense. Hard-nosed common sense will tell you that you are too wrong to meet the standards of a holy God; pardoning grace tells you that it's all right in spite of so much in you that is wrong.
>
> Realistic common sense tells you that you are too weak, too harassed, too human to change for the better; grace gives you power to send you on the way to being a better person.
>
> Plain common sense may tell you that you are caught in a rut of fate or futility; grace promises that you can trust God to have a better tomorrow for you than the day you have made for yourself.[2]

My first memory of grappling with this theological term was as a freshman at Furman University. Browsing through the college bookstore I spied the catchy title *Grace Is Not a Blue-Eyed Blonde. OK*, I thought, *I'm glad we cleared that up . . . but what is it?* It has taken me more than twenty years to answer that question, and in the answers I find myself truly amazed!

Part of my confusion came from a misunderstanding of the difference between grace and mercy. They are not the same! However, these terms are related. The best way I've found to define them is *grace is God's giving us what we don't deserve; mercy is God's not giving us what we do deserve.*

So the very nature of grace is that it is undeserved. To show grace is to extend favor to one who doesn't deserve it and can never earn it. But what do we deserve as a result of our sin and efforts to take God's place as controller of our lives? We deserve judgment and punishment. That's where both mercy and grace comes in—God in His infinite mercy does not give us the death we deserve, but as an act of grace grants us forgiveness and new life.

Having been an avid student of the modern missionary movement, I am quite familiar with that wonderful phrase "Expect great things from God; attempt great things for God." These words were first spoken by William Carey, the father of modern missions, who went to India in 1793. Not only did he translate all or parts of the Bible into more than forty languages and dialects, he was also a man of remarkable faith in God.

Imagine how surprised I was to discover recently that he, too, struggled with a full understanding of sin and grace. On his seventieth birthday, William Carey wrote to one of his sons:

> I am this day seventy years old, a monument of Divine mercy and goodness, though on a review of my life I find much, very much, for which I ought to be humbled in the dust; my direct and positive sins are innumerable, my negligence in the Lord's work has been great, I have not promoted his cause, nor sought his glory and honour as I ought, not-

withstanding all this, I am spared till now, and am still retained in his Work, and I trust I am received into the divine favour through him.[3]

Did this attitude come with the insecurities of old age? Or was William Carey suffering from what we consider a modern ailment, "low self-esteem"? Or does he reflect the healthy realism of a mature Christian? Jerry Bridges believes that Carey's attitude addresses two significant needs among all committed Christians:

> the need for humble realization of our own sinfulness, and the need for a grateful acceptance of God's grace. Christians tend toward one of two opposite attitudes. The first is a relentless sense of guilt due to unmet expectations in living the Christian life. People characterized by this mode of thinking frequently dwell on their besetting sins or on their failure to live up to numerous challenges of the Christian life.
>
> The other attitude is one of varying degrees of self-satisfaction with one's Christian life. We can drift into this attitude because we are convinced we believe the right doctrines, we read the right Christian books, we practice the right disciplines of a committed Christian life, or we are actively involved in some aspect of Christian ministry and are not just "pew sitters."[4]

We can also become self-righteous when we look around at the sin of society and decide that, because we are not guilty of these more gross forms of sin, we must be pretty good people!

Either way, we stand in need of *grace!*

Certainly one of the most gifted writers in my own generation is Walter Wangerin Jr. In his book *Little Lamb,*

Who Made Thee? he recalls his very first experience of grace. It was 1957 and he was fourteen years old, a self-appointed adult. Because it was a difficult time for his parents, Walter decided the way he could help them best was to look after his seven younger brothers and sisters and to make no demands on his folks.

But one night he was very sick, couldn't sleep, and felt terribly alone in his "adulthood."

> Now I expected absolutely nothing. It never occurred to me but that I would have to handle this misery alone. I was an adult. Free. On my own.
>
> But I must have been groaning out loud.
>
> Because suddenly the hall light came on outside my door. Then the door swung inward. And there stood my mother . . . calm, quiet, and utterly beautiful.
>
> "Wally, what's the matter?"
>
> I was stunned. This I had not expected. Her presence and her voice alone—the familiarity of a voice which I had thought I'd never hear that way again—made me start to cry.
>
> "My stomach," I sobbed.
>
> "Oh, Wally!"
>
> My mother floated toward me then and sat on the edge of the mattress, which sank to her weight. She put a cool hand to my forehead. "Yes, fever," she said. How long since she had sat beside me so? How long since she had kissed the little Wally? Long.
>
> In the dark, her hair a nimbus by the hall light, she whispered, "Pull your knees up to your tummy. It'll ease you."
>
> How holy the homely remedies! I did, and I cried and cried—for none of this should have been.

I truly never thought that I could be a child again. Oh, I thought I had lost all that.

But I had a mother, after all, and she came to me. I was exhausting myself by protecting *her* in those days, not she me—and yet she came to me. I was fully adult, independent, self-sufficient; I had forfeited the tender mercy of a mama in the night-time. Nevertheless, she came to comfort me—and like a baby I curled into the crook of her arm and wept.

This was the first and most memorable time that grace embraced me.[5]

But grace is more than "God's unmerited favor" or even "God's favor to those who actually deserve the opposite." It is a reality in life. Bible teacher Kay Arthur puts it this way, "By grace you live, by grace you please God, and by grace you are freed from religion and released into a relationship with your heavenly Father. Grace is always based on who He is and what He has done. Grace is never based on who you are apart from Him or on what you can do."[6]

Paul is the great Apostle of Grace. Of the 155 New Testament references to grace, 133 belong to him. The word *grace* is the anglicized Latin word *gratia* which was used to translate the Greek word *charis*, the word for gracefulness, graciousness, favor, or kindness.

This favor is the unexplained joy of God at giving something priceless to the totally impoverished. In other words, "Grace is God's love in action on our behalf, freely giving us His forgiveness, His acceptance and His favor. Grace is essentially a redeeming activity of God in Christ. 'For it is by grace you have been saved, through faith—and this not from yourselves, it is the gift of God' (Eph. 2:8). These words are true for the vilest and most degraded sinner; they are equally true for the ripest and shiniest saint. This grace base will never be replaced by something else."[7]

Jesus never actually used the term *grace*, but He certainly exhibited it in numerous ways. One scholar observes,

> He was never cross, never selfish, never impatient with people who had problems, never superior or judgmental. He never told people, "It serves you right" or "I hope you get what's coming to you" or "That's your problem" or "Don't bother me about it." He never disassociated Himself from anyone, as if some types or classes of people were below Him. Indeed, He moved easily among both the high and the low, and He was so much at home with the lower classes that His enemies used it to attack Him, saying that He was a "drunkard" and a "friend of sinners." People liked Jesus. They found Him gracious.[8]

One of the uses of grace in the Old Testament finds its root in an old Hebrew term which means "to bend, to stoop," eventually coming to mean "condescending favor." This is vividly seen in members of royalty who may choose to "grace" a commoner by extending a hand to the crowd. Sometimes we even use it this way sarcastically, as in "Look, Debbie has decided to grace us with her presence tonight."

The late pastor and biblical scholar, Donald Gray Barnhouse, puts it this way, "Love that goes upward is worship; love that goes outward is affection; love that stoops is grace."[9]

I love the mental picture that "stoops" evokes in my own mind. I recall the numerous times as a mother I have knelt down to my preschooler so that I could enter her world face-to-face. I didn't say to little Fiona, "Make yourself worthy and then I'll come down there and play," nor did I declare, "Because you have done this, that, or the other, I will now be with you." My stooping came as a result of my love for her and my desire to share her life and shower her with blessings.

Isn't that what God has done for us through His Son, Jesus Christ? He has condescended to enter our world face-to-face as a man (see Phil. 2) not because we merit or have earned this favor, but simply because of His great love for us and His desire to bless us.

That is the vertical dimension of grace which centers on our relationship with God. This kind of incarnational love was clearly demonstrated by a young Belgian priest and missionary, Father Damien. In 1873 he went to the Hawaiian island of Molokai to serve the more than eight thousand people of the Kalaupapa leprosy colony. These Hawaiians had been torn from their homes in the 1860s and banished to this isolated island to prevent the spread of that disease.

Father Damien nursed them, buried them, and built houses and churches in Kaluapapa. Each Sunday he would hold services, but very few lepers attended the church. Finally, one Sunday, Father Damien addressed his small congregation, "*We* lepers." He had truly become one of them. During the final years of his life, many lepers came to know the compassion of Christ through the man who dwelt among them and himself died from leprosy in 1889. For he didn't just *tell* them about Christ's grace and love, he *showed* them.

Once called upon to explain this mystery of grace, Presbyterian minister Jack Miller told this story: "Two seventeenth-century theologians were debating on the nature of grace. One said that grace is like one parent's guiding a toddler across the room to the other parent, who has an apple for the child. The nearby parent watches the youngster; if he almost falls, this parent will hold him for a moment so that he can still cross the room under his own power. But the other theologian had a different view. For him grace comes to us only in the discovery of our total helplessness. In his concept, we are like a caterpillar in a ring of fire. Deliverance can only come from above."[10]

Later, Jack Miller's wife Rose Marie shared with me that when she first heard this, she was more struck by the image of encroaching fire than by the rescue from above. I, too, have felt that way—trapped and almost engulfed with little hope of escape. But my new understanding of vertical grace is that Jesus Christ will reach down from above and rescue me. As Rose Marie says, "This is not merely supporting grace, but transforming grace."

There is also a horizontal dimension to grace which centers on our relationships with others. Only when we have totally grasped the reality of God's great gift of grace to us can we fully extend this grace to others with no hidden agenda or secret motive. Elisabeth Elliot observed, "Grace means self-giving, too, and springs from the person's own being without consideration of whether the object is deserving. [Horizontal] Grace may be unnoticed. But those who are in a desperation of suffering will notice it, will notice even its lightest touch, and will hold it as a precious, an incalculably valuable thing."[11]

After figure skater Tonya Harding successfully sued the U.S. Olympic Committee to allow her to compete in the Winter Olympics in Norway, she proclaimed, "I've worked twenty years for this! It's my *right* to skate in Lillehammer and no one can prevent me!"

Now, regardless of what you or I think about whether or not Tonya Harding *should* have skated in the Olympics, this whole real-life soap opera reveals the attitude of much of today's society. Our society believes we *deserve* certain things and we're willing (oh, so willing) to sue anyone appearing to thwart our rights. Some Christians have even fallen for this line of thinking: "If I follow all the rules and lead a good life, then God will prosper me and give me everything I deserve—success, material possessions, and good health."

Actually, we don't deserve any of these things. And, if the truth be known, it is only through God's grace that we are allowed to experience *any* blessing. All of life is a gift! That's what the Tonya Hardings of the world have missed somewhere along the way—by grace she made it onto the Olympic team and by the graces of the Olympic Committee she was allowed to skate in Lillehammer, not because it was her right, but because it was a favor they chose to grant her.

Several years ago I went through a period of my own spiritual journey which I privately refer to as "My Grace Tutorial." It seems that during those eighteen months God used every means necessary to get my attention and teach me how to live a life of grace.

One of the first things that had to go was my innate need to be in control. As long as I could maneuver people and events to work out in a desired way, then there was no need to trust God. Of course the way to resolve this was for God to give me what seemed like endless opportunities to depend on Him and Him alone. Most of those times I never deserved to be rescued, but God extended grace to me again and again until I finally understood it.

Before I was married, I traveled around the world quite a bit, usually alone. After one particularly long ten-hour flight, I landed in the airport of a poor, developing country. Our two-hour layover stretched into four without so much as an announcement. Outwardly I was seeking to project a calm business-like manner; inwardly I was about to pull out my hair from frustration. It was easy to tell who the Americans were in that waiting room—we were all at the ticket counter demanding a report!

Our third-world passengers took the situation in stride, obviously unruffled by the indeterminate delay as they calmly unpacked food and played games. About seven hours later, the plane departed—when it was ready. No amount of questions, complaints, or offers of help could get that plane off the ground! We were reduced to a posture of simply letting go and turning the situation over to those in control.

But letting go of control was most certainly not the only lesson God had for me during my grace tutorial. In fact, much of the time I learned while kicking and screaming (figuratively speaking). But in the end, His great love won out, and I began a new era in my walk of faith.

The Bible says that God is the Potter and we are the clay: "We are all the work of your hand" (Isa. 64:8). I was a potter once in the early 1970s (wasn't everyone back then?). I remember how important it was that the clay be exactly centered on the potter's wheel or it would wobble and break as soon as the wheel picked up speed. Come to think of it, my life has been a lot like that clay.

"Does the clay say to the potter, 'What are you making?'" (Isa. 45:9). I haven't always enjoyed the pounding and spinning around, the pinching off of bits of extraneous clay, or the hot furnace of the kiln which was supposed to make me strong. I'm sure I even asked the Potter once or twice if He really knew what He was making.

I now realize that grace has been a vital factor in every spiritual lesson God has taught me. And even though I'm still on the Potter's wheel, I decided to write about this journey, trusting that others might relate and perhaps be encouraged. Along the way I have discovered that this pilgrimage is an *active* one, not a passive one. So each chapter begins with an active verb, illustrating one more lesson learned the hard way in my grace tutorial.

Four autumns ago our family was packing to move from our home in Williamsburg, when my dear friend, Genelda, came over and presented me with a gift of love amidst all the chaos and confusion. She had put this verse in needlepoint and framed it in gold: "My grace is sufficient for you" (2 Cor. 12:9).

It was a promise I clung to and carried to our new home, a colonial parsonage in a small New England town. Are you surprised to know that it was the first picture I hung or that we named this home "Gracehaven"? What a wonderful reminder to each one who lives here and each one who visits that *God is enough* and He keeps all His promises.

Truly, I am amazed by grace!

◆

Amazing Applications

Why not use a notebook for your own grace tutorial and record your thoughts, observations, and answers to the applications suggested at the end of each chapter?

1. Can you think of a time when you deserved certain punishment but were granted reprieve instead? How did you feel? Did that act of horizontal grace have any effect on your further actions? Think of someone on whom you can bestow the gift of grace this week. What will you do?

2. God's grace is a gift we don't deserve. But many of us merely carry around the beautifully wrapped package and never bother to open it—to appropriate all that He has for us through His grace. Have you opened the gift? If not, why not accept God's vertical grace to you now?

3. What kind of vessel is God, the Potter, forming of you? Was it what you hoped or something totally different? Be assured that God only pounds and kneads in order to shape beauty from the rough clay. In what areas do you need to submit to Him today?

4. Read the Book of Galatians and circle each use of the word *grace* by Paul. Make a list of what you learn. How does this word study affect your own practical theology of grace?

◆

Grace Memory Verse

For it is by *grace** you have been saved,
through faith—and this not from yourselves,
it is the gift of God.
—Ephesians 2:8 —

◆

---

*Author's emphasis.

CHAPTER TWO

Afflicted in Spirit

af·'flict·ed *vb:* experiencing pain and distress

*M*ake *the world go away.* . . . I sang under my breath in my best Eddie Arnold twang. Today it was a prayer. Boy, had my morning devotions deteriorated!

It was a gray day in New England—wet, cold, and lonely. I had sent my three teenagers off to three different schools to face (among other things) the challenge of finding at least one recognizable person to sit with at lunch. No small feat when you're the new kid on the block.

My husband was off to the activity and opportunity of ministry in a growing, vibrant church. And, after settling our toddler in front of the television, I inserted a Christian Mother Goose video—good for at least thirty minutes of kid-sitting. This was something I said I'd *never* do! Maggie had celebrated her first birthday in North Carolina, her second in Virginia, and in a few weeks would turn three years old here in Connecticut.

I gulped some coffee, stuffed a bagel in my mouth without really tasting it, trudged upstairs, crawled back into bed, and pulled the covers over my head. "Make the world go away" indeed! Three states in three years! "God, do you *really* have a good plan for our family?"

Everything that goes with adapting—being strong no matter what, remaining hopeful in job interviews, organizing to move a family of six, selling houses, checking out schools, locating doctors and orthodontists and scout troops and Special Olympics teams, handling potty training and house decorating and hostessing—came crashing in on me!

With the Lord's strength I had done it all and done most of it pretty well. But now that we had settled into a comfortable routine, what little reserve I had left crumbled.

Depression had seized my soul. I, whose theme was "hope springs eternal," was acting as one with no hope. But who was I to complain? God had granted me physical health and, like the psalmist, "my lines had fallen in pleasant places" (Ps. 16:6). Yet, even so, potentially dangerous signs were surfacing because I wasn't taking care of myself. I was sick—sick in spirit.

What would make me get out of bed? I didn't just want to pull myself together to dress and have a nutritious family dinner and cheerful words when everyone returned home. I was tired of "bucking up." Band-Aids didn't work anymore—I needed surgery of the soul, and I was overdue for an appointment with the Great Physician.

Frankly, I wasn't sure if I was depressed or burnt out—or maybe a little of both. I identified with King David, "My sad life's dilapidated, a falling-down barn; build me up again by your Word" (Ps. 119:28, *The Message*). I was only thirty-eight years old and this was most definitely not how I wanted to live the rest of my life.

Like Alexander in Judith Viorst's children's story, I was having a "terrible, horrible, no good, very bad day!" Alexander's first clue that he was in for it was when he first woke up:

I went to sleep with gum in my mouth and now there's gum in my hair and when I got out of bed this morning I tripped on the skateboard and by mistake I dropped my sweater in the sink while the water was running and I could tell it was going to be a terrible, horrible, no good, very bad day. At breakfast Anthony found a Corvette Sting Ray car kit in his breakfast cereal box and Nick found a Junior Undercover Agent code ring in his breakfast cereal box but in my breakfast cereal box all I found was breakfast cereal. . . . I think I'll move to Australia.[1]

Not only have I felt occasionally like the one with the empty cereal box when God was handing out goodies, but I could relate to almost every adventure Alexander had that day, from being rejected by someone he thought was his best friend, to inadvertently making a mess at his daddy's office. But even bad days (and months and years) eventually come to an end. We just have to live through them.

There were lima beans for dinner and I hate lima beans. There was kissing on TV and I hate kissing. My bath was too hot, I got soap in my eyes, my marble went down the drain, and I had to wear my railroad-train pajamas. I hate my railroad-train pajamas. When I went to bed Nick took back the pillow he said I could keep and the Mickey Mouse night light burned out and I bit my tongue. The cat wants to sleep with Anthony and not me. It has been a terrible, horrible, no good, very bad day. My mom says some days are like that. . . . Even in Australia."[2]

Alexander's mom was right, you know. No matter where we live and with whom, there will inevitably be those days. Well, even though I was having one of them, I knew I couldn't stay under my pillow forever. So I swallowed my pride, took a deep breath, and slowly began to face my distress.

Everyone who has successfully completed any of the numerous twelve-step recovery programs can tell you in a heartbeat that the first step toward healing is to face the reality of the problem: "We admitted we were powerless over our behavior, that our lives had become unmanageable."

For me this was not as easy as it sounds. I was too deeply enmeshed in the "Pollyanna Principle"—always finding something to be glad about. This seemed right in line with certain biblical teachings on the Victorious Christian Life. If I counted my many blessings and quoted enough Bible verses ("All things work together for good. . . ." [Rom. 8:28, NRSV]), surely the blues would go away, right? Wrong.

Maybe that's why I hadn't laughed at the greeting card rack earlier in the week. The cover pictured an odd-looking lady saying "Everyone thinks I'm in denial—that I won't face my problems in life. . . ." Inside the card these words jumped out, "It's a lie!" Ouch. Maybe, instead, I should have been singing that great country hit by Pam Tillis, "Just call me Cleopatra 'cause I'm the Queen of Denial!"

"Was it really possible," I wondered, "to be a mature Christian and still be depressed?" Dr. Archibald Hart, professor of psychology at Fuller Theological Seminary, helped educate thousands of Christians, including me, when he addressed this subject on a Focus on the Family radio program. "Depression is a feeling of gloom or sadness that is usually accompanied by a slowing down of the body. It's not just in the mind, but is experienced throughout the whole body. In nearly all depression, one of the essential symptoms is fatigue. There's also a lack of energy to engage in normal activities. The sufferer becomes lethargic, lying around a lot, refusing to get out of bed or escaping into activities that make no demands."[3]

But Dr. Frank Minirth and Dr. Paul Meier also taught me something that I never knew before—depression is not just an emotional problem, but a physiological one as well. "Internalized stresses result in adrenaline release. . . . As stress continues and anxiety is not dealt with, biochemical changes will begin to occur in the body. Eventually, depletion of noradrenalin (norepinephrine) occurs. . . . Norepinephrine is a neurotransmitter in the limbic system of the brain which controls emotions such as depression or euphoria. Among other important neurotransmitters are serotonin and dopamine. . . . When these decrease to a certain level, the depression becomes physical and biochemical (in addition to being emotional)."[4]

Statistics from the National Mental Health Association reveal that 25 percent of U.S. women and 11.5 percent of U.S. men have a depressive episode during their lifetime. Small comfort. I've always hated being just another statistic. . . . How in the world did I get to this place?

To be "stressed out" has almost become a cliché these days. This past Christmas I worked in a craft shop and one day saw the arrival of a dozen cute little wooden dolls with hair standing on end and a wild expression in their eyes. Attached to each doll was a sign announcing, "Stress? What stress?" Needless to say, everyone either wanted one of those dolls for a "friend" or secretly for themselves. They did not last long on the shelves.

Some Christians even wear stress as a badge of honor—burning themselves out for God. Was I doing that? The pressure I felt was just like David Seamands describes as feeling "caught in a trap where we are expected to live up to unrealistic and impossible demands put upon us by God, ourselves and other people. And, like the hamster on the treadmill, the harder we try, the faster we run; and the faster we run, the harder we have to try to keep up with the wheel. This feeling of being trapped generates in us some strong negative emotions which keep us emotionally disturbed and spiritually defeated."[5]

As I watched our own hamster, Oreo, go 'round and 'round on his exercise wheel I realized something was deeply out of balance in my life. I had subconsciously rooted my relationship with God in perfect performance (or lack of it). I needed desperately to come to a clearer understanding of grace so that the basis of my relationship with God was Christ's perfect performance for me—His life of obedience and His death for my sins. Seamands says, "It is our trusting receptivity of the gift of His righteousness, in spite of all the sins and failures we see in ourselves, which saves us from despair and depression."[6]

Perhaps I had been in denial, but now I was ready to humbly admit that success *for* God had become more important to me than my relationship *with* God. All I wanted was to be a godly wife, a nurturing mother, and a spiritual encouragement to others through my life. Was that so wrong?

My former pastor at Wheaton College Church, Kent Hughes, describes a similar experience early in his pastoral career as he faced a shrinking church: "I was in the darkest, deepest depression of my life. My memory of this time is of a gray, horizonless sea. A faint light falls from a threatening sky and I am treading water alone, sinking. Soon I will be below the surface. Melodramatic, to be sure! But that's how I felt. I wanted out. . . ."

So Kent and his wife, Barbara, covenanted to seek a biblical view of success: "Each of us prayed earnestly, asking for God's forgiveness and freshly committing ourselves to His service. We also asked God to protect us from our cunning adversary who had so subtly seduced us."[7] Out of this journey came the very helpful volume *Liberating Ministry from the Success Syndrome*—but it would not have been written without an affliction of the soul.

After C. S. Lewis died, an anthology of his poetry was published. One poem especially, "The Naked Seed," reveals some of his own dark night of the soul and begins with saying that his heart is empty and moves on to say that his deepest desire is "to be free from pain." We all want to be free from pain, and we'll try anything, it seems, to escape it.

Patsy Clairmont is one who knows how to communicate truth in a humorous way. When I heard her speak a few years ago at a conference, her words came dangerously close to "meddling." Using her own experience, she pointed out that three common outlets for depressed Christian women are shopping, eating, and sleeping. "I slept too much. I ate too much. I talked too much. I was into unhealthy swings of muchness."[8]

Like C. S. Lewis, I, too, wanted to be free from pain. And, like Patsy, I have tried to numb the pain through "muchness." Just as I am learning how to become stronger and more balanced, so is Patsy: "For years I stumbled around emotionally hiding in different places. Feeling overwhelmed by even the dailiness of life, I tried to find comfort and safety in the shelter of my home, family members, friends and activities. . . . Since then, I have learned that we hide because we hurt, and we hurt because we don't understand how to heal."[9]

Part of our healing comes when we are able to allow the pain in our lives to make us more sensitive to the hurting ones around us. Pain is inevitable, but misery is an option.

In 1991 Dave Dravecky, former pitcher for the San Francisco Giants, had his pitching arm amputated. During his battle with cancer, his wife Jan was diagnosed as clinically depressed: "I had always been a strong person, taking care of others. In fact, I used to feel guilty if I'd take time for me. I saw independence as a strong Christian virtue. After all, Galatians 6:2 tells us we're to bear one another's burdens. But the Greek word for 'burden' means 'boulder'—something too heavy to carry alone. My problem was I wasn't letting anyone carry my boulders, yet I was carrying everyone else's."[10] Jan now hopes to help other women who suffer from depression. She and Dave have encouraged many through their book *When You Can't Come Back* and the Dave Dravecky Foundation.

When I was afflicted in spirit, I turned to Christ. I sought His face, I devoured His Word, and I asked Him to mend the broken pieces of the life I'd messed up so badly by trying to be good. I often turned to the poetry of Christina Rossetti, particularly a small volume given to me by a friend in seminary:

A Better Resurrection

I have no wit, no word, no tears;
    My heart within me like a stone
Is numbed too much for hopes or fears;
    Look right, look left, I dwell alone;
I lift mine eyes, but dimmed with grief
    No everlasting hills I see;
My life is in the falling leaf;
    O Jesus, quicken me.

My life is like a faded leaf,
   My harvest dwindled to a husk;
Truly my life is void and brief
   And tedious in the barren dusk;
My life is like a frozen thing,
   No bud nor greenness can I see:
Yet rise it shall—the sap of Spring;
   O Jesus, rise in me.

My life is like a broken bowl,
   A broken bowl that cannot hold
One drop of water for my soul
   Or cordial in the searching cold;
Cast in the fire the perished thing,
   Melt and remold it, till it be
A royal cup for Him my King:
   O Jesus, drink of me. [11]

As God infused my own life with hope and healing, I became increasingly aware of people who were hurting around me. They had been there all along, but I was perhaps too wrapped up in myself to notice. One week I received three letters in the mail: Trina was grieving her best friend's sudden death as well as coping herself with a serious medical diagnosis; Jed, father of two toddlers, had just discovered his wife's lapse into prescription drug addiction and was striving to hold his marriage and family together during Mom's four-month absence at a treatment center; and Margaret, married to a minister for twenty years, was wondering where she and the kids would live now that her husband had divorced her to be with one of his mistresses.

I was overwhelmed. These people were all believers who had spent their lives serving God and others. Never in a million years would they have suspected life would turn out this way. I wish I could say this was an atypical week, but the next week I heard from Lucy whose husband lost his job on the same day she discovered her baby had Down's syndrome; two different women (one young, one not-so-young) showed up at my door with experiences of spousal abuse; and my college friend, Bev, went jogging one day only to return home to find her husband inexplicably dead in their yard. Could God's love and grace touch these lives? And could I somehow be a channel through which He worked?

As one who surrounds herself with books, it was only natural for me to glance up at a book that had sat unopened on my shelf for several years. That day it practically jumped off the shelf. Kay Arthur's *Lord, Heal My Hurts* had been a farewell gift from one of our former parishioners. Unfortunately, when I received it, I was too much in the middle of my hurts to find the emotional energy to do a Bible study on the subject. Perhaps the time was right now. . . .

I knew that evening Bible studies for women had thus far not been entirely successful at our church. Nonetheless, I placed an announcement in the church bulletin that I would be teaching a fourteen-week Bible study on "Lord, Heal My Hurts." Then I prayed.

By the first night sixty-five women had committed to the course and paid for a book. Fifty of us lasted the entire fourteen weeks. I made it clear the first night that this was not fourteen-easy-weeks-to-get-rid-of-all-your-pain. Instead, we would be studying God's Word, getting to know the heart of Jesus, praying, and in the middle of all that, the healing process would unfold. And that's just what happened.

There's a story told about Ruth Bell Graham which reveals both her wisdom and her sensitivity. One day she visited the shop of a man who specialized in piecing broken pottery and china back together. Mrs. Graham's desire was to buy something with one piece still missing. When the craftsman showed surprise, she explained to him that his activity reminded her of God's work in human life. "God," she said, "carefully and lovingly takes the broken pieces of our lives and glues them back together again."[12]

I can testify that God does mend the broken pieces of our lives—but He often leaves a small crack or chip as a reminder that we are indeed "wounded healers." Like the psalmist, "It was good for me to be afflicted so that I might learn your decrees. . . . for I have put my hope in your word" (Ps. 119:71, 74b).

Perhaps your particular affliction is not personal but results from watching a loved one go through pain. God's word of grace would encourage you to never give up, never stop loving and being there for your dear one. Sometimes all we can do is pray, but that very prayer is the power of God to change lives. ____

Monica's heart was broken as only a Christian mother's heart can be. When her son reached adolescence he began to follow in the footsteps of his pagan, lustful, violent father. She wanted to see him settling down with a godly wife, but instead he moved in with a mistress and they had a son. Monica begged her son to join the church and take hold of the life-changing truths of Christ, but instead he fell in with a cult and dabbled in dark heresies.

The young man moved to Rome and when his mom tried to follow him, he tricked her into missing the boat. He thought he could escape her, but he didn't realize the power of her prayers and perseverance. This mother prayed for fifteen years and every day she went to church to pour out her heart to God. Monica never lost confidence that her prayers for her son would be answered.

Finally the young man repented and gave his life to Christ. And it was a good thing too! For Monica lived from 331–387 and her son was named Augustine (known to us as Saint Augustine). Because of a mother's prayers this brilliant theologian's passion for God and profound spiritual wisdom shaped the entire course of Western civilization.[13]

Listen to his response to God as recorded in Saint Augustine's *Confessions:* "Too late I loved Thee, O Thou Beauty of ancient days, yet ever new! Too late I love Thee! And behold, Thou wert within, and I abroad, and there I searched for Thee. . . . Thou calledst, and shoutedst, and burstest my deafness. Thou flashedst, shonest, and scatteredst my blindness. Thou breathedst odors, and *I drew in breath* and *pant for Thee.* I tasted, and *hunger and thirst.* Thou touchedst me, and I burned for Thy peace" (italics his).

No doubt someone is praying for you, perhaps right now. I know that many have prayed me along life's journey—prayers that I didn't deserve, but prayers given out of a heart of grace. I'm farther along the road now than I was that horrible, terrible, no good, very bad day when I only wanted to hide under the covers.

One fellow pilgrim sums it up this way: "The road to emotional well-being is a winding road, similar to the one the Israelites walked on their way to the Promised Land. We may uncover some giants, a plague or two and a few pits. But we will also climb mountains, munch manna and, with His help, gain some life-changing views."[14]

The journey of a lifetime begins with one small step.

◆

Amazing Applications

1. Depression can have several causes: emotional, spiritual, physical, or even a combination. If you have been depressed for several months, consult a medical doctor to determine if there are physical problems. For many, depression is manifested in an inability to function

normally in the home or at work—just not finding pleasure anymore in daily living. Don't hesitate to consult a Christian counselor or psychologist who can help you get perspective and emotional healing.

2. Read King David's words in Psalm 42, particularly verses 5–6. Meditating on Scripture, such as this psalm, can be an antidote to affliction. How do these words apply to a situation you now face? Take some time this week to focus on God's ability and desire to help you rather than your own inability to help yourself.

3. If you don't keep a journal, you might want to start. Writing down prayers and concerns sometimes helps give perspective. Describe a painful experience, a time of spiritual affliction. It may be something in the past or something you are in the middle of right now. Do you believe God is with you in the middle of this pain? Read Psalm 13 and meditate on His loving character and His desire to bring healing into your life.

4. Are you in a place you feel no one else has ever been? Believe me, someone has. Ask your pastor to recommend a "survivor" who would be willing to meet with you and give you hope. Or go to a Christian bookstore and check out the biography section for those who have lived through affliction. Remember that pain is inevitable, but misery is an option. Make a decision now, by the grace of God, that you will not opt for misery.

◆

Grace Memory Verse

My *grace* is sufficient for you,
for my power is made perfect in weakness.
—2 Corinthians 12:9—

◆

CHAPTER THREE

Approved in Christ

ap·'proved *vb:* accepted and regarded favorably

I cried a little each day for the first four months of 1981. I didn't cry due to homesickness—although I *had* just moved to California, three thousand miles from family and friends. I didn't cry due to increased work demands—although becoming Missions director at a 4,500-member church *did* have a tendency to overwhelm. And I didn't cry due to challenging relationships—although I *had* discovered a small group who had lobbied for their friend to get my position. Why did I cry?

I cried for fear of failure.

It was the early 1980s, the *me* decade, and our congregation was located in the heart of Silicon Valley near Stanford University. Success was all around and I, for one, was dizzy. "Here at Menlo Park, the staff is free to succeed!" a fellow pastor remarked with a twinkle in his eye. It was a joke. But I didn't get it.

Our senior minister, Walt Gerber, was one of my first encounters with a Christian who makes himself vulnerable in order to minister from weakness, not strength. All around us lives were being touched and healed. The church was full of grace and acceptance. But I was still young and far too full of a need to prove myself in this latest in a long line of life's risks. So I worked hard at pioneering a new ministry which, by the grace of God, became a national prototype for local church involvement in missions by the time I left four years later.

Still, I had not yet learned the importance of paradox in a Christian's life—that to gain my life, I must first lose it; that for seed to grow, it must first be buried. I was still grappling with Paul's words: "Am I now trying to win the approval of men, or of God? Or am I trying to please men? If I were still trying to please men, I would not be a servant of Christ" (Gal. 1:10).

No, in my twenties I had not yet fully recognized the grace of God's unconditional acceptance of me. I was still striving to earn His approval. But my years in Menlo Park were preparing me. And I *would* learn. "I tell you the truth, unless a kernel of wheat falls to the ground and dies, it remains only a single seed. But if it dies, it produces many seeds" (John 12:24). Oh yes, I most certainly would learn . . .

I was born in a beautiful little town in south Georgia into a society where "being nice" is a cultivated art form. The magnolias and azaleas bloom in profusion, but so do the words—words that heal, but also words that hurt. Part of me is very thankful for a heritage which encouraged friendliness, hospitality, and enthusiastic affirmation. But there is also a part of me that recognizes how important *approval* is in the Deep South (and probably most every-where else, too, if the truth be known).

From the vantage point of age, I now realize that there was pain and failure and loneliness among many I encountered—those who projected an everything-is-just-fine demeanor in public. To be approved of was success; to experience disapproval meant to be ostracized. Having experienced a little of both in my young life, I decided to leave town a year early. I crammed all the necessary senior courses into summer school just after my junior year and unceremoniously received a diploma in August. Barely seventeen years old, I began a new chapter in my life as a college freshman in another state.

I found great freedom in those years. Since no one had known me before, there were no preconceived expectations of me, and I was free to find my own way. But as my personal faith in Christ grew deeper I realized I had been too often playing the same game—only this time I was trying to win approval as a *Christian*. I had simply exchanged one kind of approval (social status) for another (the Christian milieu). Achievement in that world soon became my barometer for self-acceptance. Was I reading the *right* theology books, becoming active in the *right* causes, wearing clothes that made the *right* statement of my chosen lifestyle? Yet I did all of this out of a genuine love for Christ!

How do we believers get off track so easily when we know we aren't set right with Christ by rule keeping but only through personal faith in Christ? It is a comfort to me to realize I am not alone in this struggle. Even Saint Paul spoke about this two thousand years ago:

> What actually took place is this: I tried keeping rules and working my head off to please God, and it didn't work. So I quit being a "law man" so that I could be God's man. Christ's life showed me how, and enabled me to do it. I identified myself com-

pletely with Him. Indeed, I have been crucified with Christ. My ego is no longer central. It is no longer important that I appear righteous before you or have your good opinion, and I am no longer driven to impress God. Christ lives in me. The life you see me living is not "mine" but it is lived by faith in the Son of God, who loved me and gave Himself for me. I am not going back on that.

Is it not clear to you that to go back to that old rule-keeping, peer-pleasing religion would be an abandonment of everything personal and free in my relationship with God? I refuse to do that, to repudiate God's grace!

—Galatians 2:17–21, *The Message*—

The good news is that Christ approves of me! The bad news is that I have to break a lifelong habit of thinking I must somehow *do* something to win that approval. Being a "Type-A" personality, I tend to be intensely focused and rarely content to do anything halfway (well, except maybe housecleaning, but that's for another book . . .). So I'm usually going 100 percent—that is, unless I'm totally burnt out and can't do anything!

When I'm burnt out, I worry. I've been told that worrying betrays a distinct lack of trust in God. That worries me too. Sometimes I feel just like Erma Bombeck:

I've always worried a lot and frankly, I'm good at it. I worry about introducing people and going blank when I get to my mother. I worry about a shortage of ball bearings; a snake coming up through the kitchen drain. I worry about the world ending at midnight and getting stuck with three hours on a twenty-four-hour cold capsule. I worry about getting into the *Guinness World Book of Records* under "Pregnancy: Oldest Recorded Birth." I worry what the dog thinks when he sees me coming out of the shower; that one of my children will marry an Eskimo who will set me adrift on an iceberg when I can no longer feed myself. I worry about salesladies following me into the fitting room, oil slicks, and Carol Channing going bald. I worry about scientists discovering someday that lettuce has been fattening all along.[1]

Pretty ridiculous, eh? Most of all, we worry about whether or not people would really accept us if they knew what we were *really* like. Barbara Goodyear described it this way:

> Who will accept me? We rejoice when we hear God say "I have loved you with an everlasting love; I have drawn you with loving-kindness" (Jer. 31:3). We go to Him and let Him show us who we are. Then we will not try to extract our security and self-esteem from other people. People can help meet our needs for belonging, but they can never be the spring from which we drink for self-esteem and security. That comes only from a relationship with God.[2]

A message on my flip calendar tells me that the most dangerous heresy on earth is the emphasis on what we do for God, instead of what God does for us: "Many claim that their favorite verse of scripture is 'God helps those who help themselves' (which doesn't appear in the Bible). Talk about killing grace! The fact is, God helps the helpless, the undeserving, those who don't measure up, those who fail to achieve His standard."[3]

My husband, Mike, reminds me every time I speak, "Remember, Cindy, you are speaking to an audience of ONE!" It is Christ's approval alone that matters. But, of course, the reality is that I *do* care about what others think. There is, however, quite a difference between God's job and mine: "God's job is to fix and change. Our job is to depend, serve and equip. This is the work of grace. And it is more restful than you can imagine."[4]

Most Christians I know (including myself) would love to rest in the assurance of God's love and approval. Why, then, do we feel so driven? It is because many of us have spent our whole lives *striving* instead of embracing the grace that would give rest to our souls. But sometimes it takes a major upheaval to force us to stop and "smell the roses."

In 1984, after ten years of active ministry around the world, a most *remarkable* thing happened to me. At the age of thirty-one I had the joy of marrying a wonderful Christian man—Michael McDowell! Marvelous as it sounds, marriage was a serious decision for me. Mike had been a widower for three years and had just returned from overseas ministry with his three small children.

I prayed, sought godly counsel, and finally believed then, as I do now, that this marriage was part of God's plan for me. Frankly, I didn't want to blow it. My desire was to be the best wife and the best mother in the whole world! I willingly resigned from my career and moved from San Francisco to Seattle to embrace my new life as an at-home mom. I wanted to make life better for Mike and the children after their years of grief.

Could I really have been so naive? This time I gave 110 percent! Since the kids had been without a mother for three years, I thought it only natural to make up for that by serving as room mother in three different schools, as a Cub Scout den mother, and also a Brownie Scout troop leader. I instigated swim lessons, home Bible studies, library and reading enrichment—I even took a class for mothers of handicapped children at the nearby university so I'd know how to advocate for Justin, our oldest son who was born mildly mentally retarded. And to help them feel more a part of a new church, I began giving weekly children's sermons. Whew! All this in the early stages of marriage and motherhood!

This was the real me, just too much of it. But one great observer of life would have suggested perhaps I was motivated by a part of me he calls the Impostor: "Impostors are preoccupied with acceptance and approval. Because of their suffocating need to please others, they cannot say no with the same confidence with which they say yes. And so they overextend themselves in people, projects, and causes, motivated not by personal commitment but by the fear of not living up to others' expectations."[5]

Let's face it—I was trying hard, too hard I realize now. With all the factors involved—new marriage, instant motherhood, new geographic location, new church, new career, etc.—I made quite a few mistakes. I desperately wanted approval from my husband, to show I could be just as good a wife as, if not better than, his late wife to whom he had been married ten years. I also wanted approval, love, and acceptance from the children. Not to mention approval from my new in-laws, Mike's colleagues and friends, the world I had left behind and, in general, just about everyone!

In reality I carried around a certain feeling of failure whenever Mike and I would disagree on parenting or I'd become frustrated and impatient with children who were simply acting like children. Then, one day in desperation I spent a quiet day at "Stillpoint" retreat house. There Jesus met me in my disillusionment and told me to stop worrying about how I appear in the eyes of others. Instead, I began to daily seek His face, striving to be faithful only to what He clearly called me to do.

Eleven years later, upon hearing my story, one lady remarked to me, "I don't know how you did it!" (Because, quite frankly, Justin, Tim, and Fiona are pretty terrific young adults now . . . no prejudice, mind you.)

Without blinking an eyelash, I looked straight at her and declared, "*I* didn't do it. God did. Justin, Tim, and Fiona are who they are today not because of me, but in spite of me. It's merely grace—*all grace*."

Once while interviewing Elisabeth Elliot for a magazine article, I asked, "What do you want to be remembered for?" Surely with her list of credentials—author of more than twenty-eight books, host of a daily radio program, international speaker, wife of slain missionary Jim Elliot, mother of one, and grandmother of eight—I expected her to have to think about her answer, but she was alarmingly quick with her reply, "I have no ambition except to be a faithful servant. If I can hear from God, 'Well done, good and faithful servant,' that's all I care about really."[6]

I, too, hope to have that attitude one day, but find that I am not alone in the pursuit of it. Ruth Senter writes about a conversation with her heavenly Father: "Yes, Lord, I am forever tired in my efforts to *do* love. It is a full-time job. Sometimes my hands do not move heartily in the service of Your Love . . . the clock ticks on and my guilt grows. So much to do. So many to serve. So much harvest not yet in."

But she also writes of God's reply: "Sometimes, child, you seem to have a hard time letting Me love you. It seems easier for you to scurry around doing love than to open yourself to letting Me love you. . . . I am not surprised that you are wearied by the doing of love. When you think you can do all the loving, you *will* get weary. When you cannot receive, you *will* soon have nothing to give. . . . You don't have to be anything for Me except what you are, My child. *You are Mine.* Everything you are and everything you are not. Give Me your best, yes, but don't stop there. Give Me your worst as well. I am big enough to handle both."[7]

I'm usually eager to give my best, but in recent years I have also been able to give God my worst. And you know what? He can handle both! Secure in that knowledge, I am more real and obedient, leaving the results to God. Yes, I still care about what people think. After all, I'm only human (and Southern at that). But others' expectations no longer drive me. *Success is not as important as faithfulness.* God has been right beside me in every triumph of my life. But I have also experienced dismal defeat only to find Him there as well.

Kevin Miller noted, "God's love doesn't depend on our performance. It depends on Jesus Christ. The reason Jesus stretched out His arms on the Cross was so He could reach them around people like you and me. . . . If you experience God's love at your lowest moment, you'll know it has nothing to do with your condition—and everything to do with God's amazing grace."[8]

Christian psychologist Larry Crabb says that each person has a need to feel that he or she is making a difference in life. What I am discovering is that, in Christ's eyes, I *am* making a difference.

I *am* approved, simply because I *am His.*

◆

Amazing Applications

1. Are you a people pleaser? Sometimes what appears as pressure from others ("I'd better perform because people expect it of me") is actually pressure from ourselves ("I'd better please people because I want them to like me"). Give up people pleasing! After all, you can never

please everyone. To what important request this week can you say no politely?

2. Next time you are involved in introductions, try to say who you *are* instead of just what you *do*. (It's hard, isn't it?) Conversely, when you meet someone new, try to ask questions that will help you get to know the person inside, as well as all the peripherals. This is one way of showing that you, like God, put value on other than performance. How would you introduce yourself?

3. Is your Christian life more a religion of rules than a relationship with a living Christ? Are you paralyzed by guilt and a sense of failure when you make a mistake in your Christian walk? Please read Galatians 2:17–21. If Christ lives in you, then know beyond the shadow of a doubt that you have been saved by grace, not by works! To what "rules" are you submitting yourself?

4. Ask yourself the same question I asked Elisabeth Elliot in my interview, "What do you most want to be remembered for?" As you ponder the answer, think also about what changes need to be made today in order to accomplish it.

◆

Grace Memory Verse
I do not set aside the *grace* of God,
for if righteousness could be gained through the law,
Christ died for nothing!
—Galatians 2:21—

◆

CHAPTER FOUR

Astonished by Sin

as·'ton·ished *vb:* <u>stricken</u> with sudden wonder

*I*n the privacy of the lodge's conference room, the counselor from Philadelphia looked straight into my eyes and said, "Cindy, you are a very angry person."

"Me, angry? How preposterous!" I exclaimed, while thinking to myself, *This man just met me. What does he know?*

Frankly, it made me furious!

But since I've always tried to examine whatever truth might lie in an admonition from a fellow Christian, I calmed down and began to think. Could there be just a small kernel of truth here?

"Uh, I guess I have stuffed a lot of feelings—disappointment over unmet expectations, grief at losses, guilt from failure and resentment when things seem unfair . . ." I trailed off.

"But that's just it!" he pointed out. "Situations left unresolved and struggles not yet surrendered to the Lord build up inside, only to be eventually released in unhealthy ways. Anger is merely an emotion. There's nothing wrong with the emotion itself but the Bible says, "'In your anger, do not sin': Do not let the sun go down while you are still angry" (Eph. 4:26).

I swallowed hard—struck to the core by the Holy Spirit. While that verse acknowledged that we can expect to experience anger, it also pointed out that how we handle our anger is the important determination of whether or not it will lead to sin.

My own anger was merely a symptom of yet unnamed sins—pride, lack of trust in God, self-centeredness. My sin was blatant every time I chose to go my way and not God's way. Why trust when I could worry? Why surrender when I could control? Why show compassion when I could stand in judgment? Why accept responsibility when I could blame others?

Bible teacher Cynthia Heald defined sin as "whatever weakens your reason, impairs the tenderness of your conscience, obscures your sense of God, or takes off the relish of spiritual things; that thing is sin for you, however innocent it may be in itself."[1]

In the past I had publicly witnessed, "I am the sinner for whom Christ died." But how little I had truly believed it . . . until now. I wept in the sheer astonishment of how utterly undeserving I was of God's forgiveness and pardon—of His grace.

Sin is not a very popular word in our culture today. According to Brian Abel Ragen, "Our culture does not believe in wickedness—that is, in culpability. The 'conviction of sin' is hardly possible to us. We believe not in sin and forgiveness but in illness and recovery. It is the endless message of our culture that everyone is basically good and that most of our problems will be solved when we realize this—in other words, when we build up our self-esteem."[2] But self-esteem is not enough!

Psychologist Larry Crabb says that personal diagnosis is always unpleasant for sinful people. No wonder that counselor's words cut me to the core! But diagnosis, no matter how deflating, must precede treatment, because it informs us what treatment is needed and makes us gratefully willing to receive it. Crabb said, "There is no such thing as 'easy' confession. True confession is always an agonizing process. Brokenness over personal sin is a necessary step in learning to love graciously."[3]

Becky Pippert captured my experience perfectly when she wrote, "Jesus died and we crucified Him. And the Good News is that because of the price God was willing to pay we can be forgiven and reconciled back to God. But to experience the benefit from the cure we must turn to Him and quit pretending there is nothing wrong with us. That is true sacrilege, pretending that there is nothing wrong with us when it cost God the life of His Son to rectify our problem. God's mercy and justice are finally reconciled through the cross. Why did God take such dramatic effort to rescue us? Because He wanted to forgive us so much. And the amazing thing is, we did not even know we needed it."[4]

I had never thought my sins were all that bad, certainly not as bad as those criminals on the evening news. But my former Sunday School teacher, Joe Bayly, warned of just such thinking. "People in general, Christian people in particular, tend to divide sins into two categories: their sins and our sins. The Bible, of course, knows no such distinction. Sin is sin, without partiality shown to the sins of God's people—our sins."[5]

It has been suggested that believers are sometimes willing to accept certain "refined sins" such as a judgmental spirit or that old favorite, gossip. Others might be in the area of interpersonal relationships—resentment, bitterness, an unforgiving spirit, impatience, and irritability. Jerry Bridges says, "One of our problems with these so-called refined sins is that we have become too comfortable with the whole concept of sin. Because we do sin so frequently we learn to coexist with it as long as it doesn't get too out of control or scandalous. We forget, or perhaps have never learned, how seriously God regards all sin."[6]

Until I was astonished by my own sin, I was unable to be amazed fully by the grace God freely offered me. From my heart knowledge (and not just my head), I literally sang out the words of a hymn by Horatio Spafford:

> My sin, oh the bliss of this glorious thought
> My sin, not in part, but the whole
> Is nailed to the cross and I bear it no more
> Praise the Lord, praise the Lord, Oh my soul!

And so the journey continued—out of anger into adoration, from fear to forgiveness. After my encounter with the counselor, I spent that afternoon making a list of all my known sins and confessing them to the Lord. I even confessed quite a few to my husband. There was, however, one thing left to do.

At sunset I took a walk along the Chesapeake Bay where I was staying. Completely drained from the catharsis of the day, I looked out into the water and suddenly remembered Corrie ten Boom's words: "Jesus takes your sin—past, present and future—dumps it in the ocean and puts up a sign that reads 'No Fishing Allowed!'"

After picking up a large stone, I walked to the end of the pier. As an autumn wind blew and tears ran down my cheeks, I prayerfully threw the stone into the bay.

Do I still need to daily confess my sins? Yes—even though I am a new creation in Christ, the Holy Spirit has come to dwell within me, and I have been freed from the dominion of sin. Despite this I still sin and must repent daily, as well as accept forgiveness daily.

But I'm also learning the freedom of keeping short accounts with the Lord—no more stuffing and festering! To commemorate my "Beth-el" I hung a tiny framed picture in our bedroom. It shows in vivid shades of gold and orange a small pier jutting out into the sunset of the Chesapeake Bay—my pier and a daily reminder of old hurts confessed, forgiven, and now buried deep.

To live by grace means to acknowledge my whole life story, the light side and the dark. In admitting my shadow side I learn who I am and what God's grace means. As Thomas Merton put it, "A saint is not someone who is good but who experiences the goodness of God."

Why is it that when the veil lifts in one area, other areas also come more sharply into focus? I don't know. But I do know that after this revelation in my own life, I became extra sensitive to similar struggles in the lives of others. One of the most encouraging testimonies came from my friend, Sarah. Thousands of miles away, God was simultaneously working in her in similar ways.

Sarah had exceptional "credentials" as a Christian (if there are such things). She was born into a strong Christian family, graduated from a Christian college, served with her husband in Christian camping ministry for nine years before they went to the mission field. She was a devoted wife and mother of four. But during her seventh year in South America spiritual doubt, physical stress, and emotional turmoil forced her to be astonished by her sin.

Home on furlough, she was led by a gracious God into a study of Galatians. One day Sarah was radically changed while driving down the highway and memorizing a personal version of Galatians 2:20: "I, the hypocritical Sarah, will no longer live but Christ lives in me, and the life I now live in the flesh, I live by faith in Christ who loves me and gave everything for me." For the first time in her exemplary Christian life, Sarah knew God's love for her was based on what Christ did on the cross—taking her sin onto Himself and giving her His righteousness.

In 1992 she wrote me from Bolivia:

> I am a different person. I am no longer agitated and driven by fear or guilt. My soul feels like a calm river; no matter what circumstances overwhelm me, inside I know the peace of God. My daily, frequent sins are obvious to me now, whereas before I was blind to them. Seeing them, repenting of them, frees me from their hold over me. It is AMAZING! I do not have to be obsessed with myself, *my* family, *my* worries, *my* plans, *my* needs, *my* wants, *my* questions, *my* abilities or limitations. *Me*-ness does not have to rule me any more. I am hungry for the Bible and for more of God's forgiveness and love.
>
> I never knew that Christ could change someone like me—someone who looked all together, with a good husband and happy family, no major problems from the past or present, living a life serving God. But I was dying inwardly with the cancer of self-centeredness and pride. And I didn't even know it! I never knew how blind I was to my daily sin and self-righteousness and helplessness. I never knew how much I needed God. I never knew His great salvation and acceptance in Jesus Christ. I never knew it was this true.

My favorite radio preacher, Steve Brown, loves to remind his listeners that "Jesus didn't condemn bad people. He condemned 'stiff' people. We condemn the bad ones and affirm the stiff ones." He goes on to relate the story of the Anglican priest who saw an elderly woman who, because of the thought of her sin, shrank from drinking the communion cup. The priest finally stuck it under her nose and said, "Take it, woman! It's for sinners! It's for you!"[7]

Have *you* had this moment of truth yet? Magazine editor Mike Yaconelli wrote of a time when he retreated to the L'Arche community in Canada to find solace but, instead, found his true self. "Finally I accepted my brokenness. . . . I had never come to terms with that. Let me explain. I knew I continually disappointed God, but I could never accept that part of me. It was a part of me that embarrassed me. I continually felt the need to apologize, to run from my weaknesses, to deny who I was and concentrate on what I should be. I was broken, yes, but I was continually trying never to be broken again—or at least to get to the place where I was very seldom broken. . . . I came to see that it was in my brokenness, in my powerlessness, in my weakness that Jesus was made strong."[8]

This is what happened to me. Until I faced my own sin and brokenness, I could never fully grasp the magnitude of God's love and grace. Or as one recovered alcoholic says, "We cannot receive what the crucified Rabbi has to give unless we admit our plight and stretch out our hands until our arms ache."[9]

Perhaps the essence of sin is a preoccupation with ourselves. Some of us start with self-*importance* while others wallow in self-*worthlessness*. But either way, we become all important, either due to our own prominence or insignificance.

Mother Julian of Norwich once made the statement, "Sin will be no shame, but honor." Brennan Manning, no stranger to the sin in his own life nor to the unconditional love of his Father, elaborates: "The lives of King David, Peter, Mary Magdalene, Paul, along with contemporary witnesses such as Charles Colson, lend support to Julian's paradoxical statement. They all found their capacity for evil, harnessed the power, and by grace converted it into a force for something constructive, noble and good. This mysterious grace is the active expression of the crucified Christ who has reconciled *all* things in Himself, transforming even our evil impulses into part of the good."[10]

Throughout my life I have memorized the words to hundreds of hymns. I find that closing my eyes in worship (and not relying on a hymnal) helps me to focus on Christ and the meaning of the words I'm singing. Many hymns reduce me to tears, but none so much these days as the second stanza of Augustus Toplady's "Rock of Ages":

> Could my tears forever flow,
> Could my zeal no languor know,
> These for sin could not atone;
> Thou must save, and Thou alone:
> In my hands no price I bring,
> Simply to Thy cross I cling.
> Rock of Ages, cleft for me,
> Let me hide myself in Thee.

When the truth conveyed in these lines is finally etched on our hearts, then, and only then, will we truly experience and embrace the grace of God.

◆

Amazing Applications

1. "If we claim to be without sin, we deceive ourselves and the truth is not in us" (1 John 1:8). Do you have a hard time facing and repenting of the daily sin in your life? Why not try what I did—write a list and in a moment of repentance and consecration offer your sins, past and present, up to the Lord. Keep a reminder on your desk or in your journal of this special experience.

2. In Psalm 51 King David faced his own sin with Bathsheba (after a little help from Nathan). Do you feel that your sin is unpardonable? Read Psalm 51 and find hope. No sin is too great to be forgiven! Of course, while God does forgive us, He does not always erase the natural consequences of our sin—David's life and family were never the same again after what he had done. Perhaps you may never meet that baby you once put up for adoption, you may have to serve prison time for embezzling, or reconciliation with your divorced spouse may be impossible due to the other's remarriage. Regardless, from now on you can have new life.

3. Have you ever harbored a judgmental attitude toward others? Did you recognize that as sin in your life? Take time now to ask forgiveness for the times you did not offer grace but instead jumped to condemnation. The more you face your own need of forgiveness from sin, the more natural it will be for you to extend horizontal grace to others.

4. Try memorizing the words to one of the hymns from your church's hymnal. Make a copy, or better yet, buy yourself a hymnal—it should be a constant companion in your devotions. Practice singing in your car or as you work. You may just discover that learning hymns by heart helps you worship in a more focused way.

◆

Grace Memory Verse

See to it that no one misses the *grace* of God
and that no bitter root grows up to cause trouble
and defile many.
—Hebrews 12:15—

◆

CHAPTER FIVE

Adopted by God

a·'dopt·ed *vb*: taken as one's own child

*I*t was a hot July day as we drove across the Evergreen Point Floating Bridge to Ravenna Park in Seattle. I fingered the corsage Mike had given me and thought of what lay ahead. We were on our way to the courthouse.

Although in my early thirties, I had never actually been to court before—except, of course, for "helping" Perry Mason and Della Street solve hundreds of cases. But then, that was criminal court; we were only going to civil court. Still, I didn't know what to expect, and it made me nervous.

There was much gaiety and activity as we stopped at the park to pick up three young children from our church day camp. I had mothered these children for awhile, and now I would become their legal mother. All the interviews and paperwork had finally been completed. I was adopting Justin Thomas Gregory McDowell, Timothy Michael

Laurens McDowell, and Fiona Johanna Yvonne Mc-
Dowell.

Their first mother, Inka Van Seventer McDowell, had
died from liver cancer four years earlier. Although we had
never met, I felt very close to her as I made this significant
commitment to raising her children.

In cleaning our attic the week before, I discovered a
small plaque containing a prayer in Dutch, her native
language. Fortunately, Inka had written the English translation on the back only a few months before her cancer was
discovered:

Prayer for My Children

I lay the names of my children in Thy hands.
  Engrave them there with unerasable writing,
That nothing or nobody can ever burn them out
  of there, even if later Satan sifts the wheat.
Hold Thou my children if I have to let them go
  and let Thine power always stand above their
  weakness.
Thou knowest how ruthless the world will hate them,
  if they do not follow the rules of the world.
I am not asking Thee to spare my children all sadness
  but be Thou their comfort if they are
  lonely and afraid.
Do keep them in Thy covenant for Thy name's sake,
  And let them never estrange from Thee,
  never, their whole life long.
I lay the names of my children in Thy hands.
  Amen.

—Geeske Wiersma—

Tears had filled my eyes as I read. God in His mercy
had somehow chosen me to marry her children's father and
play a major role in their Christian nurture. Feeling terri-

bly inadequate I clung to the promise: "The one who calls you is faithful and he will do it" (1 Thess. 5:24).

. . . And now, my day in court! My father-in-law, a strong Christian attorney, was there to guide the way. Judge Epstein ushered us into a small room (which, by the way, looked nothing like Perry Mason's courtroom!). Nine-year-old Justin, noticing the judge's long black robe, asked, "Are you our pastor?" Our laughter broke the ice. The ceremony was short, but we chose to celebrate festively with Grandpa and Grandma McDowell who had warmly embraced me into their family. We even mailed printed adoption announcements which included this verse "Here am I, and the children the LORD has given me!" (Isa. 8:18).

But there were a few surprises too, especially when the judge handed us the children's newly revised birth certificates. All three had been born in Seattle, but on the line for "mother" was now printed *Lucinda Lee Secrest* and my place of residence at the time of their births.

In 1975, when Justin was born, I lived in Raleigh, North Carolina, and worked as a magazine writer—my first job out of college. When Timothy was born in late 1976, I was living in Montreat, North Carolina, working as a rehabilitation teacher for blind people in twenty rural counties. And on Fiona's 1979 birthday my residence was Wheaton, Illinois, where I served in communications for the Lausanne Committee for World Evangelization—my first job after graduating from seminary.

How odd to remember each of these chapters in my life—how adventurous and carefree they had been! Little did I know that even as these three tiny babies were entering the world, God was preparing me to become their Mama. Is it then no wonder that, to me, adoption seems like a holy event—whether one is adopting or being adopted?

Seattle attorney David V. Andersen is deeply moved by what his law practice has encountered in recent adoption cases. He says, "I have begun to see in the lives of the adoptive families I work with a picture of God's love—for others and for me. I have concluded that recovering a biblical theology of adoption can help us know more about God and experience Him in new and vital ways."[1]

In order for a new family to be created, the former structure must be dissolved. Even the birth certificates must be altered. In our case, we've also saved the original birth certificates and our children are very aware of "Mommy Inka" and her life, even though they have few actual memories. We have all remained close to her six brothers and sisters through the years, as well as to our seventeen Dutch nieces and nephews. This summer, two of Inka's sisters will holiday at our home.

The gift of my children is certainly one of the most tremendous acts of God's grace in my life. I have done nothing to deserve them and I have not earned the right to be their mother. Nonetheless, God chose to grant me the great privilege of having two sons and two daughters. By the time our fourth child, Margaret Sarah Secrest McDowell, was born five years later, we had truly bonded as a complete family. And although I must have had a life before kids, I just don't remember much about it!

"To be adopted ultimately depends upon the choice of someone else," David Andersen observed. "Only parents can petition to adopt a child, not vice versa. Paul says that God chooses us to be His children. He also says that the motivating force behind this choice is love."[2] How well this is illustrated in the framed picture I saw recently which said, "If flowers were daughters, I'd pick you!"

Being a parent has given me an understanding glimpse into one of the most significant truths of God's Word: "For in Christ Jesus you are all children of God through faith. . . . But when the fullness of time had come, God sent his Son, born of a woman, born under the law, in order to redeem those who were under the law, so that we might receive adoption as children. And because you are children, God has sent the Spirit of his Son into our hearts, crying 'Abba! Father!' So you are no longer a slave but a child, and if a child then also an heir, through God" (Gal. 3:26, 4:4–7, NRSV).

Even though I don't possess great material wealth, all I have is fully available to my children. Because of my great love for them, I willingly give of my resources, my strength, my creativity, my wisdom, my encouragement, and my possessions each day. Once they were not my children, but now they are. How sad I would be if they acted as though I'd never come along! How useless I'd feel if they never came to me for all the blessings I so desire to give them. But if I feel this way, how much more so must my heavenly Father feel when I run around acting like an orphan and not as an adopted child of God!

All we who have chosen to live for Christ are sons and daughters of the King! We are His heirs and thus have access to all He is and all He has to bestow on us. Wouldn't my day go differently if I began each morning looking into the mirror and proclaiming, "Cindy, you are the daughter of a King! Now live like it!"?

"How great is the love the Father has lavished on us, that we should be called children of God! And that is what we are!" (1 John 3:1). What great news this is for any who never knew the love of an earthly father, the care of a mother, the safety of a home. How special to know we no longer need to wander around on our own.

Author Brian Chapell put it this way:

> To know whether you are a child of God, do not ask whether your life is sinless, but whether

your heart is Sonlike. Do you still long for His love? Do you grieve for His hurt? Do you ache for the pain of Him who gave His only Son for you? When your spirit cries out in love for your heavenly Father, then it testifies of the Spirit of God in you that marks you as a child of God. Such love leads you to the Father in new confession, new obedience, and new assurance of your relationship with Him, despite past failure. When the heart cries out, *"Abba, Daddy,"* the heavenly Father experiences joy and the child's heart knows peace.[3]

In 1850 as many as thirty thousand immigrant orphans lived on the streets of New York. With no money and no relatives, they slept in alleys and survived by stealing. Only Charles Loring Brace, a twenty-six-year-old minister, cared enough to organize a solution—the Orphan Train. It was described like this:

The idea was simple: pack hundreds of orphans on a train leading West and announce to towns along the way that anyone could claim a new son or daughter when the Orphan Train chugged through. By the time the last Orphan Train steamed West in 1929, 100,000 children had found new homes and new lives. Two orphans from such trains became governors, one served as a United States Congressman and still another was a U.S. Supreme Court Justice.[4]

As these children, whose parents had perhaps died on a ship immigrating to the United States, were adopted into new families, how real Paul's encouraging words must have seemed to them: "You are no longer foreigners and aliens, but fellow citizens with God's people and members of God's household" (Eph. 2:19).

Jack and Rose Marie Miller of World Harvest Mission were perhaps the first to drive the truths of "sonship" home in my heart. One of the first stories Rose Marie ever told me was of a time during a mission trip to Uganda when she felt spent and empty. Later, when Jack spontaneously called on her to witness at a large outdoor gathering of Africans, she faithfully went through the motions, but she left feeling defeated.

Walking with her husband a few days later, Rose Marie exclaimed, "Why couldn't I cope and love people?"

God spoke very clearly through Jack's answer, "Rose Marie, you act like an *orphan*. You act as though there is no Father who loves you and no Holy Spirit who comes to help you live in impossible places and do impossible things!"

With this revelation came a whole new purpose in Rose Marie's life—to help others learn to live, not as orphans, but as sons and daughters of God. I wouldn't be writing this chapter if I hadn't, in God's mercy, been the recipient of such teaching.

I learned that when I act like an *orphan* I have certain characteristics. I act as though

♦ I am all alone and therefore it is all up to me.

♦ I am full of felt needs but want help from no one.

♦ I live on a success/fail basis.

♦ I am full of fears and have little faith.

♦ I am defensive and a poor listener.

♦ I have a complaining and thankless attitude toward God and others.

♦ I feel trapped by circumstances and that no one cares.[5]

But if I live in the knowledge and freedom of a *daughter/son* I display entirely different characteristics:

- I have a growing assurance of God as my Father because of a true understanding of the Cross.
- I'm building a life partnership with God based on the gospel and not self-effort.
- I'm more forgiving, less judgmental and condemning.
- I rely on the Holy Spirit to help me use my tongue for praise and not complaint or gossip.
- By faith I see God's sovereign plan over my life as wise and good.
- I learn to pray, claiming the promises of God.
- I seek daily forgiveness and cleansing from my sins.[6]

One of my biggest problems was forgetting to find my identity through God's love, acceptance, and grace. It seemed more natural to cling to achievement which was, of course, fleeting and fickle. But when I'm secure in my identity as a daughter, "whether I fail, succeed, change, resign, or get fired or promoted doesn't matter. We are God's own, His children, members of His everlasting family, the objects of His unconditional love. And He bought us with the blood of His very own Son Jesus Christ. What else really matters? Nothing. Everything else pales into insignificance when compared to that."[7]

To think of God as a father figure can sometimes be an obstacle in the path of faith. This is particularly true for those whose own fathers were distant or even abusive.

When Ingrid Trobisch came to speak at our church several years ago, she mentioned that her late husband, Walter Trobisch, had been given the special privilege of helping students worldwide come to a truer understanding of God the Father.

Snowbound during a blizzard, she and I drank tea while she told me how she had learned the sense of safety and belonging with her heavenly Father.

"I remember sitting on my father's lap when I was a child—he was a kind and good father. I was sixteen when he died and that's a hard time to lose a parent. But it was only a tiny step for me to find my heavenly Father and give myself to Him. Sometimes it also takes another fatherly man to teach us to recognize our value. My own three uncles helped affirm me. It is almost impossible to become a confident woman without affirmation. I can't fathom a single day in my life when I don't figuratively crawl up into the lap of the Father and let myself be loved."

Do you ever crawl up into your Abba's lap and let yourself be loved? It was quite unusual for Paul to invite us to address God with the most intimate term of "Abba" or "Daddy." How wonderful that Jesus Christ, the Son, did not hoard this experience for Himself, but invited us to share in this intimacy: "For you did not receive a spirit of slavery to fall back into fear, but you have received a spirit of adoption. When we cry, 'Abba! Father!' it is that very Spirit bearing witness with our spirit that we are children of God" (Rom. 8:15–16, NRSV).

Brennan Manning says the greatest gift he ever received from Jesus Christ was the Abba experience.

> On that radiant morning in a cabin hidden deep in the Colorado Rockies, I came out of hiding. Jesus removed the shroud of perfectionist performance and now, forgiven and free, I ran home. For I knew that I *knew* Someone was there for me. Gripped in the depth of my soul, tears streaming down my cheeks, I internalized and finally felt all the words I have written and spoken about stubborn, unrelenting Love. That morning I understood that the words are but straw when compared to the Reality. I leaped from simply being the teacher of God's love to becoming

Abba's delight. I said goodbye to feeling frightened and said shalom to feeling safe.[8]

I began this chapter with a story about a hot July day in Seattle where I came to see adoption as a holy process. I'd like to end it with another hot day in July ten years later. This time, in the New York Adirondacks, my own Abba experience was once again reinforced through a "splendor in the ordinary."

The new playground at *Camp of the Woods* was dedicated on July Fourth. And what a playground it was! Bright orange, royal blue, and electric yellow edifices of every imagination—tunnels, swaying bridges, wavy slides, bars, and swings.

At least one hundred children joined in the grand celebration. Occasionally my husband and I caught sight of our daughter's red, white, and blue shirt or her American flag hair bow.

Five-year-old Maggie was delighting in a world of discovery when suddenly she came upon it—the fireman's pole! We watched as she looked down from the landing, carefully calculating whether or not she really wanted to leap out and slide down on her own.

I felt it coming long before I actually heard the word. "DAAAAADDY!" Her shriek was lost in the cacophony of play, but one man heard it. Mike rushed quickly to her side and supported her little body as she bravely attempted to slide down the pole.

With fear gone, Maggie explored each piece of equipment, but every time she reached the fire pole platform she hollered, "DAAAAADDY!" to the masses, and Mike rushed to her rescue. She couldn't see us on the sidelines and didn't need to for most of her play, but she knew her daddy was there. When she called out to him, she knew he would make her feel safe.

As a very interested bystander, I marveled at this vivid picture of my own life being played out by my youngest child. For I, too, am the child of an attentive and caring Daddy.

How utterly grateful I am that God is my Father. Much of the time I'm all too content to carry on with the health, gifts, and resources He has graciously chosen to give me.

But more and more often these days, I perch on a precipice, ready to risk it all in one giant leap of faith. My hastily uttered prayer, "Dear Father" sounds strangely like Maggie's shrieks of "DAAAAADDY!" And, like her, no sooner do I cry out than "underneath are the everlasting arms."

It's a promise I can count on. And I do.

◆

Amazing Applications

1. "How great is the love the Father has lavished on us, that we should be called children of God! And that is what we are!" (1 John 3:1). As a child, what place gave you a sense of security and haven? Do you have a "safe place" like that now? Would you like to? In your greatest time of loneliness and need this week, close your eyes and imagine yourself sitting in the lap of the Heavenly Father. Imagine His loving you and holding you tight. Rest in His love.

2. Do you sometimes act like an orphan? Review the list of orphan characteristics and pick one that you would like to eliminate from your life. Look up Scripture on that subject and make that characteristic a special matter of prayer this week. You'll be delighted at what your Father will do!

3. Even if you never had the kind of parents who gave you unconditional love and security, you can be that kind of parent for your own children. Do you show your children love, both through words and actions? Have you made it clear that your love is not contingent upon their behavior, but merely because they are your children? Think up something creative to do for each individual child that will be a picture of your love reflecting the love of the heavenly Father. (If you have young children, you might want to read aloud Max Lucado's *Just in Case You Ever Wonder.*)

4. Do you feel comfortable calling God "Daddy"? If not, write Him a letter explaining why this is a difficult thing for you. Then pray that you will be able to embrace the Abba experience in your own life.

◆

Grace Memory Verse

So that, having been justified by his *grace*,
we might become heirs having the hope of eternal life.

—Titus 3:7—

◆

CHAPTER SIX

Assaulted by Doubt

as·'saulted *vb:* violently attacked

*T*he seminary professor from California found his seat on the plane and was pleasantly surprised to see the man next to him praying. Delighted at the prospect of sharing the journey with a Christian brother, he commented, "Hello. I couldn't help but notice that you were praying. I'm a Christian too!"

His seatmate looked up startled. "Oh, I'm not praying to *God*. I worship Satan—I'm praying to *Satan* today."

Recovering from his shock, the Christian professor managed to mumble a few words, "Well, what are you praying about?"

With a smile on his face, this perfectly ordinary looking young man replied firmly, "I am praying that Satan will destroy all the Christian ministers in New England!"

I literally gasped when my husband told me this story. Mike had just returned from a pastors prayer summit where forty New England ministers gathered specifically to pray and worship for three days.

"Truly we are in a battle against principalities and powers, Cindy," Mike said seriously. "The enemy is not pleased with people finding new life in Christ. We must arm ourselves for spiritual battle."

I admit that the awareness of spiritual warfare has only surfaced in my life in recent years. Before, I'd been content to relegate it to missionary stories or the charismatics who seemed to be extra sensitive to that sort of thing.

But as I got older, it became impossible to ignore biblical warnings: "Be self-controlled and alert. Your enemy the devil prowls around like a roaring lion looking for someone to devour. Resist him, standing firm in the faith, because you know that your brothers throughout the world are undergoing the same kind of sufferings" (1 Pet. 5:8–9).

Now a prowling, hungry lion was something I had already encountered firsthand, and it was not a pretty sight! Years before when I had visited my friend, Anne, in Kenya, we had awakened at sunrise one morning on safari. As our jeep happened upon a "kill" in process, our guide proclaimed, "Do you know how lucky you are to see this today?" One peek at the lion tearing into the helpless gazelle and I slumped down in my seat knowing that breakfast would be a lost cause. So *this* is what Satan wants to do to *me* today!! No thanks.

Spiritual warfare is a fact of life because of Satan's rebellion against God. Since the fallen angel knows he'll never be like God, he pours all his diabolical force into "devouring" his enemies—God's children. The root meaning of the word *devour* is "to swallow." Satan would like nothing better than to swallow us up in our own worries and doubts, rendering us helpless for the kingdom.

Steve Brown wryly observes, "Satan doesn't come up and say 'Hi, I'm the devil, and I'm going to destroy you!' He comes as a mysterious stranger, as one who cares, who understands, and who's willing to listen. Then he attacks, often subtly, but always viciously. . . . When you've had a mountaintop experience and then sinned, have you ever had the thought, 'If you really are a Christian, you wouldn't do that'? You didn't get that thought from God. Satan likely planted that lie in your mind."[1]

Some years ago Mike and I sustained a blow in ministry which opened the door to assaults of doubt. At the risk of over-simplifying a complex situation, let me just say that unclear expectations mixed with growing pains in a young church forced Mike to make a decision to change pastorates. It was one of the most painful chapters in our family's life. Even our relationships with colleagues and friends became strained. It's no wonder that in our disappointment and perplexity, doubt began to creep in.

From the vantage point of time I can now share that, in God's grace and mercy, He brought us incredible joy and opportunity—"beauty from ashes." But at the time, when our emotional wounds lay open to all, I believe Satan almost, but not quite, robbed us of hope.

David Seamands addresses this very issue in *Healing for Damaged Emotions*: "Satan's greatest psychological weapon is a gut feeling of inferiority, inadequacy and low self-worth. This feeling shackles many Christians, in spite of wonderful spiritual experiences and knowledge of God's Word. Although they understand their position as sons and daughters of God, they are tied up in knots, bound by a terrible feeling of inferiority, and chained to a deep sense of worthlessness."[2]

Almost everyone struggles with these feelings at one time or another. The great accuser loves to discourage us and make us want to give up. Timothy Warner says, "The two most foundational truths that come under attack are the character of God and the identity of the believer as a child of God through faith in Jesus Christ. Once a person's concept of God is perverted, his concept of what it means to be a child of God is affected. This sometimes takes the form of blaming God for all the bad things that happen in life. It also takes the form of believing we have to reach a certain level of perfection before God will accept us. Since people may not live what they profess but will always live what they believe, success in spreading these wrong beliefs gives Satan an inroad in the most foundational area of our lives—our hearts."[3]

At some age each one of my children has asked me in one way or another, "Mama, does the devil have a lot of power?"

"Yes," I always reply. "The devil does have power and the forces of evil are real and nothing to fool around with!"

But then with a twinkle in my eyes, I conclude. "But always remember, God has *more* power and we know that Christians have the final victory."

My own mama always told me, "The best way to resist temptation is to stay out of temptation's way!" Paul puts it this way, "Do not give the devil a foothold" (Eph. 4:27).

In order to make us feel crushed and crummy, he plans a battle in our minds. I know this to be true.

After speaking at a women's conference in Vermont, I stayed near the front of the room to be available for prayer and counsel. One particularly attractive senior citizen came forward and surprised me with her tearful words, "Please pray for me. I have terrible blasphemous thoughts about God." I did pray with her and felt helpless to do much more since I was soon leaving for home in Connecticut.

A few days later I received a letter from Rosalie telling me that those thoughts had greatly lessened. She went on to say that everything began when she wondered what blasphemy meant. It first occurred decades ago when she lived alone and had too much free time. Satan entered and it became an ongoing problem. For several years the thoughts left. But sometimes Rosalie had them in church right out of the blue! . . . She closed the letter by asking me to pray for her deliverance from evil thoughts forever.

Tom White, president of Frontline Ministries, says the evil one plays dirty and is quite adept at projecting thoughts into our minds. "If you regularly wrestle such intrusive thoughts as doubt about God's goodness, fear of condemnation, feelings of worthlessness and despair, you may indeed be the tempter's target. If depression, negative thinking, or anxious thoughts plague you and you can't shake them, exercise your scriptural authority to resist the lies of the enemy. Stand firmly on God's promises and tell the devil, *'I'm a blood-bought, sin-cleansed saint of God—get off my back!'*"[4]

Warren and Ruth Myers, Navigators staff members in Singapore since 1970, learned firsthand about God's powerful weapons for use in spiritual battle when their eighteen-year-old son, Brian, was taken captive by Satan. He didn't get involved in Satan worship, the occult, drugs, or sex. But he did fall under the influence of existentialism, agnosticism, and nihilism—modern philosophies that drive many young people to commit suicide.

"This ushered us into one of our longest, most traumatic periods of spiritual warfare. As years crept by, God used truths from His Word to rescue us from fear and unbelief," the Myers recalled.[5]

Perhaps the most helpful Scripture for those of us in the battle is "Put on the full armor of God so that you can take your stand against the devil's schemes. . . . Stand firm then, with the belt of truth buckled around your waist, with the breastplate of righteousness in place, and with your feet fitted with the readiness that comes from the gospel of peace. In addition to all this, take up the shield of faith, with which you can extinguish all the flaming arrows of the evil one. Take the helmet of salvation and the sword of the Spirit, which is the word of God" (Eph. 6:11, 14–17).

Ruth Myers remembers, "As we watched Brian drift away from God, Satan would assault us with thoughts that we had failed as parents. I would combat this with the truth that God had blotted out my past failures.

"These pieces of armor (from Eph. 6) represent basic elements in our walk as obedient Christians. We are safest when we meditate often on Ephesians 6 and use it as a prayer list and a checklist—a reminder to choose the thoughts and actions consistent with each piece of armor.

"As we prayed, we sought to focus our prayers on God's purposes and glory, not on our own impatience or our preferences. In His own way and time, God delivered Brian from these satanic philosophies into a life that continues to glorify the Lord."[6]

Maybe you've never played with the fire of deception and cults. But perhaps you can remember a time when you had a really big dream—only, before you even started to accomplish your goal, you were consumed with fear of failure. Or maybe you felt compelled to give an expression of love and caring to someone but never followed through because you let yourself be discouraged that your gesture wouldn't be accepted. Where did those thoughts come from?

Lloyd Ogilvie, chaplain of the U.S. Senate, calls Satan the original put-down artist! He says, "He seeks to counteract Christ's positive conditioning of our thinking. His goal is to get us out of the spiritual battle. He is too clever to launch a frontal attack. Instead, he sneaks behind the lines of our defenses, tries to minimize our vision, and causes us to be satisfied with the mediocre—and even base—things in life. His strategy is to get us to settle for less than the best the Lord wants us to have, to distract us from our King's optimal plan for us, the people around us, the church, our communities, and our nation."[7]

One clergy couple from the Northwest discovered this the hard way. Unable to reconcile some marital problems, they spent several months in counseling with a fine Christian psychologist. He worked hard. They worked hard. But progress was slow.

Then one day the counselor said, "I don't quite understand it. You are both committed Christians seeking to do God's will in your lives and marriage. You've absorbed everything we've addressed in our sessions. But we've hit a wall. It seems there is a force at work seeking to come between you. I strongly suspect a spiritual attack of some sort."

Bloodied but unbowed, the couple had hung in there for years when the wife told me their story. Through her tears she asked, "Is *this* what happens when we try to live faithfully and touch our world for Christ?"

My answer to her was steeped in reality, "Yes, sometimes it is." Because spiritual warfare is real and sometimes even the best soldiers take "bullets" and fall down in defeat. And do they always invite these "bullets"? Heavens, no! Often they are the targets of a premeditated strategy intent on neutralizing them and all those they touch.

Gordon MacDonald, senior minister of Grace Chapel in Lexington, Massachusetts, had plenty of time to think of such things when he lay on a spiritual battlefield from wounds he thought would never heal. "For me there were some 'medics,' some healers who were uniformed in grace. They found me and determined I should recover to fight the battle another day. Today, years later, I receive many phone calls from wounded soldiers who have experienced spiritual warfare from the dark side. For them spiritual warfare is no longer a cliché; it's a reality. And they need grace-driven stretcher-bearers, healers, and cheerleaders who believe not only in spiritual warfare but restoration and are committed to getting them back up to fight again.

"Christ-followers must go all the way: if we speak of spiritual warfare with seriousness, warning one another of an enemy who ambushes and takes good people captive, we must also have a strategy to rescue those taken hostage or left wounded on the battlefield."[8]

When Steve Brown was growing up, a bully moved into his neighborhood. Much older and bigger, the guy scared Steve to death. But Steve eventually decided that the only way to get the bully off his back was to stand up against him. So Steve stood his ground. "Much to my surprise, he became scared. He started to tremble all over! I said to myself, 'Man, I'm really something!' Then I heard a noise and turned around to notice my father, standing behind me on the front porch. I hadn't terrified that bully, but the presence of my father sure had. It's the same way for us as believers. Except our Father isn't standing *behind* us—He's active *in* us through the presence of His Son and the power of His Spirit. Who could ever challenge Him and win? No one, not even Satan and all the powers of hell. The devil doesn't stand a chance!"[9]

Brian Chapell warns us, "When God's people tremble before Satan, he wins. God tells us to be aware of Satan but not to fear him. Fear paralyzes us. Awareness arms us. We see the truth about Satan in God's Word, not on a movie screen, nor in the latest novel on the occult, even if it appears in Christian trappings. . . . God promises that even if the evil of this world takes us as sheep to slaughter, nothing can separate us from the love of Jesus. Satan's reach always exceeds his grasp. He cannot conquer God nor defeat God's plans. We are to see the reality of Satan's attacks, but we are never to be blind to who is sure to win. Christ will be the ultimate victor of every spiritual war."[10]

Consider these words penned by Martin Luther in "A Mighty Fortress":

> And though this world, with devils filled,
> should threaten to undo us,
> We will not fear, for God has willed
> His truth to triumph through us.

I, too, have sustained a few wounds in the battle. But I wear them with gratitude and grace as I limp forward, hopeful and alert.

Amazing Applications

1. Have you ever felt the assault of the enemy? We are warned in Colossians 2:8, "See to it that no one takes you captive through hollow or deceptive philosophy, which depends on human tradition and the basic principles of this world rather than on Christ." What are some practical ways you can fight these subtle temptations? Start by monitoring your television, movies, music, magazines, and books. Know that evil disguises itself as an "angel of light," and the media can be a great tool for dispensing such falsehood. Ask God to give you a spirit of discernment.

2. Look up 1 John 4:1–6 and write down how to test the spirits to see whether they are from God. Be aware that sometimes doubt and low self-confidence can render us helpless. But that passage also reminds us that "greater is He that is in you than he who is in the world."

3. How can God's presence in your life help you to resist Satan? Write down your answers so you will be

prepared. Realize that when the attacks come you usually have no time to think.

4. Prayer is a mighty tool against the enemy. Covenant with the Lord to pray daily and fervently for your spouse, each of your children and grandchildren, and others in your life. Pray that each one will be protected from Satan's deceptions and will have the spiritual strength and maturity to stand firm.

◆

Grace Memory Verse

Let us then approach the throne of *grace*
with confidence, so that we may receive mercy
and find *grace* to help us in our time of need.
—Hebrews 4:16—

◆

CHAPTER SEVEN

Assisted in Freedom

as·'sis·ted *vb:* helped or aided

T he weight of the backpack was cutting into my shoulders. It was heavy—too heavy. But after all, I had filled it with enough gear for two weeks on the trail. Groaning and stumbling, I heard words that were music to my ears, "Okay, everybody, five minutes rest!"

Instead of collapsing on the ground (which is what I wanted to do), I leaned against a large boulder, resting the extra weight on it. I knew if I actually took off my backpack, I would never get it back on again!

I had enrolled in this seminary course "Wilderness Training for Christian Maturity" hoping to be stretched physically, mentally, and spiritually. Boy, was I getting my money's worth! In addition to backpacking through the Adirondacks for two weeks, we also experienced a two-day solo in the woods, made a litter to carry out an injured hiker, and studied Dietrich Bonhoeffer's *Life Together*.

But the real test for me was rappelling down the side of the one-hundred-foot cliff. The fear I carried was a burden much heavier than my pack. Since I am a control freak by nature, the thought of backing down a cliff on belay (connected only by rope to my leader) put the fear of God into me! I guess that was the point.

It was the ultimate trust test. Could I truly let go of my secure position on the cliff and leap backwards with the faith that veteran mountain climber Gerry would stand firm?

I had never been so frightened before in my life. But it finally boiled down to this: I wanted the freedom of rappelling more than I wanted the security of *terra firma*. So I took a deep breath and . . . soared. Once I caught the rhythm it wasn't hard at all. I felt so free bouncing down the mountain and was almost (but not quite) disappointed to reach the bottom so quickly.

Are you a slave to fear? Does anything or anyone hold you in bondage? Do you truly want to be *free* more than you want to be *secure* in the status quo? In the article "When You're Afraid of Things That Haven't Happened Yet," Carol Kent asserts: "God created each of us with the ability to choose if we will stay frozen in fear and allow our anxieties to get out of proportion to the actual danger, or if we will move forward. Though no one can go back and make a new start, anyone can start now and make a brand-new end. It's never too late!"[1]

Author Dr. Susan Jeffers maintains that we need to do something—anything—to keep from being frozen in our paralyzing fears: "Say yes to life. Participate. Move. Act. Write. Read. Sign up. Take a stand. Or do whatever it takes for you. Get involved in the process. . . . Whatever it takes to get you there, *feel the fear and do it anyway*."[2]

I recently participated in the "Faithlift" conference near Boston where Carol Kent was the keynote speaker.

Carol is a poised and glowing speaker who is positively the last person I'd guess was ever in bondage to fear. And yet, she travels the country sharing about her own struggles to tame the deep fears inside. This truly delightful communicator loves to remind us that while fear is energy draining, the surrender that leads to faith-filled decision making is energizing and freeing. She says, "God has given me a choice—stay frozen or get moving toward taming my fears. Instead of getting stuck in the process, I can choose to get help."

Kent continues to share how she has been assisted in freedom: "The surprising result is that a yielded inner spirit always leads me to feel grief for the phobia that has held me in bondage. This sorrow brings me to a brokenness before God. As I yield my will to Him and experience true surrender, I find a strength for my current situation that I never had before. And with that strength I am empowered to make faith-filled decisions."[3]

For years, my friend Mary carried the weight of having been raised in an alcoholic home. One of her greatest fears was never knowing what normal was. "I decided that if I could just find out what normal was, I would be safe. . . . After I became a Christian, I made a marvelous discovery: God's grace—His unfailing love for us—is the constant power at work in every believer's life. *Grace is the norm of Christianity.* Like the hurricane winds that could not be seen except by their effects on the trees, grace is understood by its effect in our lives."[4]

One weekend there was an open house at Northern Correctional Institute, the new maximum security prison in Somers, Connecticut. More than six thousand people toured the stark facilities, commonly known as "Super Max." No expense had been spared to make this prison escape-proof for the most hardened criminals who were soon to take up residence there.

During the evening news, the local TV camera took me on a tour of the cells. I imagined what it would be like to spend twenty-three hours each day (prisoners are allowed one hour in a somewhat larger area) in that tiny cubicle. And how preposterous it would be for a prisoner, once freed, to willingly go back to Somers!

And yet, we do the same thing everyday. The resurrected Christ has freed us from the burden of sin and fear and performance. Why, then, do we insist on living as prisoners?

"Formerly, when you did not know God, you were slaves to those who by nature are not gods. But now that you know God . . . how is it that you are turning back to those weak and miserable principles? Do you wish to be enslaved by them all over again?" (Gal. 4:8–9).

Our old master definitely doesn't want us to read these verses. Chuck Swindoll says, "He wants you to exist in the shack of ignorance, clothed in rags of guilt and shame, and afraid of him and his whip . . . *That* is heresy! Because our Savior has set us free, the old master—the supreme grace killer—has no right whatsoever to put a whip to your back. Those days have ended, my friend. You're *free!*"[5]

Because my church was first "gathered" in 1635, I often think back to the countless "cloud of witnesses" who once worshiped there. Our current sanctuary was built in 1761 and is still called *The Meetinghouse* because, in those days, all important events in town took place at church. The members of First Church of Christ Congregational in Old Wethersfield at that time were quite staunch supporters of the patriot cause. They wanted their freedom from England!

Historian Lois Wieder explains, "They likened England's persecution of her colonies to the Old Testament persecution of the Hebrews by the Egyptians; encouraged their people to enlist and to support all resistance efforts;

and when war actually came, saw divine intervention in all colonial victories."[6]

She notes one historic document that recounts "the Sunday following the Lexington alarm was a busy one in Wethersfield. The Broad Street or First Company of the Sixth Militia regiment prepared to march to Boston. They attended the morning service as a body and sat in the gallery. 'Dr. Marsh preached and everyone in the church was in tears.' Final preparations were made and in the afternoon families and friends gathered in front of the meetinghouse where Dr. Marsh offered a prayer."[7]

During the Revolutionary War, General George Washington worshiped at my church three times. Sunday, May 20, 1781, was particularly notable because it was during the meeting Washington had with the Count de Rochambeau to plan the Battle of Yorktown. The following Tuesday the generals and their aides met in Old Wethersfield to hold what has been called "the most important conference of the war."[8]

When I worship in the meetinghouse, I can't help but wonder: "Is this the pew where George Washington sat"? My mind imagines that Sunday when so many of the parishioners were coming for spiritual sustenance before embarking on a journey from which they might never return. Were they excited? Were they exhilarated? They were going to fight for *freedom!* And they were willing to lay down their lives for freedom if that were required.

St. Paul wrote, "It is for *freedom** that Christ has set us free. Stand firm, then, and do not let yourselves be burdened again by a yoke of slavery. . . . You, my brothers, were called to be free. But do not use your freedom to indulge the sinful nature; rather, serve one another in love" (Gal. 5:1, 13).

*Author's emphasis

Christ did not die so that we would be more burdened! As Brian Chapell wrote in his book, *In the Grip of Grace*:

The faithlessness that burdens all prior to conversion results from failure to believe in Christ's pardon. But the faithfulness that still burdens many Christians results from the failure to receive Christ's pardon. There is no benefit and no merit in denying the effectiveness of Christ's sacrifice for our sin. *God's desire is that we would be free of the weight of our sin so that we can be released to serve Him fully.* Christians should rejoice in the forgiveness that frees from guilt, not wallow in the guilt that they hope will purchase forgiveness. Only the blood of Christ purchases our pardon, and that purchase has already been made. If God, as the highest judge, says our worst sins are forgiven because of the work of his Son, then we have no right to condemn ourselves. Rather, we have the privilege of confessing past sin and the responsibility of expressing present joy for the pardon he has already purchased.[9]

I am reminded of an excellent 1986 film, *The Mission*, which tells the true story of Jesuit priests ministering to the Indians of Argentina, Paraguay, and Brazil in 1750. Jeremy Irons played the brave priest who risked everything to bring Christ to the jungle people "above the waterfall." Actor Robert DeNiro portrayed the mercenary, Captain Rodrigo Mendoza, who had spent his life killing and enslaving those very same Indians. In a jealous fit of rage, he killed his own brother in a duel. Faced with his sin, he retreated into solitude for six months and then was recruited by the priests to return to the Mission San Carlos above the falls.

Perhaps the most poignant scene was of Mendoza spending days climbing the rugged terrain, rocky cliffs, and dangerous ravines with the other priests. For, you see, he had tied onto his body a large cargo net full of the vestiges of his old life—very heavy swords, armor, and guns. His climb was tortuous and took every ounce of his strength. Halfway through the journey the priests could not stand it any longer. Father John, played by Liam Neeson, shouted to Jeremy Irons, "How long must he carry that stupid thing?"

The father replied, "Until *he* believes he has carried it enough."

Finally, covered in mud and exhausted from the strain, Mendoza staggered into the Indian village with the priests and collapsed. The Indians recognized him as the killer he once was, and for a tense moment they held a threatening knife over the head of this almost defeated, broken man.

But instead of cutting his throat, they cut off the burden and tossed it over the waterfall. Mendoza broke down in tears of relief and repentance. He was finally free!! The Indians laughed at him crying and, one by one, came up to hug him. As the scene ended, Mendoza was crying one moment, laughing the next, embracing the forgiveness of the Indians and of the merciful God who had gloriously set him free.

"What burdens from your past are encumbering you as you journey up life's road?" I asked several hundred women at a retreat after I had shared this movie.

Jesus issued a two-fold invitation to all his followers when He said, "Come to me, all you who are weary and burdened, and I will give you rest " (Matt. 11:28). We are invited to be with Him, and we are invited to bring our burdens along. The first part of the verse and invitation focuses on the Lord and His desire for our company. The second part focuses on us and our needs for rest and freedom. Through prayer we can respond to both invitations and that's what I was moved to do on that retreat.

I decided to end that session in silence, giving the participants a free hour to go and "do business with God." The Holy Spirit had convinced me that there were many burdens in that room that needed to be laid at the foot of the cross. I wanted so much for those dear folks to experience freedom!

Weeks later I received a letter from Catie:

> Your messages before the meditation time touched me so—everything I had been dealing with, I finally wanted to let go of it all. Married at eighteen, I was abandoned by my husband when our second child was six months old. With a three-year-old and a baby, life was pretty dismal. I turned from God and started living for parties. I am lucky—every step of the way I felt guilty! I could not harden my heart against my Lord. I tried to be a mom and work and still keep up the pace for night life. All this time I was hating the kids' dad more and more! This isn't how it was supposed to be.
>
> Then I met my second husband—another mistake. This guy was into sadomasochism. He abused me physically and mentally. It took me six months to get away. And only when I left did my daughter tell me of his visits to her room. . . . Oh how I hated him! I eventually ended up in New England where I found a 'priceless gem'—my husband, Al.
>
> But at the retreat, I finally left it all at God's feet—the shame, the hurt, the hate, even the guilt. Everything is there. I walked up the mountain spring and prayed. I prayed harder than I ever have and tears flowed down my face. As I watched the water rush by, I sent each burden in my life down

that stream. I talked to God about each person I hadn't forgiven—about my shame, suffering, and pain. I feel whole. I feel *free.* Thank God for that retreat. Thank God for you.

Have you carried around a backpack full of fear, shame, and unforgiveness? Wouldn't you love to be free from all that extra weight? Perhaps the best known illustration of these truths is found in John Bunyan's *Pilgrim's Progress.* The pilgrim's original name was "Graceless" and we follow him and his burden through many trials to the Celestial City. Known now as "Christian," he is finally free of the burden he has carried so far.

And who took that burden from him? Christ, of course, when He took our place on the cross. Can you imagine ever willingly taking the punishment for someone else? For our children we would certainly be willing to give our lives, and perhaps even for other loved ones. But what about a perfect stranger? What kind of grace does it take to free another?

In his book *The Body,* Chuck Colson shared the gripping story of one man who did just that in the hell of Auschwitz concentration camp during World War II—Father Maximilian Kolbe. Father Kolbe, a Polish monk, was only forty-five years old when Nazis captured him and thousands of other Polish priests. At Auschwitz, priests didn't live very long because the SS officers made them carry whole tree trunks from one place to the other. When Kolbe, weakened from hunger, slipped and fell, he was beaten and left for dead.

When he recovered somewhat, he was moved to Barracks 14 where he continued to minister to the prisoners so tortured by hunger that they could not sleep. But one day, as a result of one prisoner escaping, the rest of Barracks 14 was ordered to stand motionless at roll call

all day. In the evening, with all the other prisoners witnessing, the commandant announced the terrifying sentence: "Ten of you will die for him in the starvation bunker!"

Colson recorded the scene:

The starvation bunker! Anything was better—death on the gallows, a bullet in the head at the Wall of Death, or even the gas in the chambers. All those were quick, even humane, compared to Nazi starvation, for they denied you water as well as food. The prisoners had heard that . . . the condemned didn't even look like human beings after a day or two. They frightened even the guards. Their throats turned to paper, their brains turned to fire, their intestines dried up and shriveled like desiccated worms.

As the commandant chose the ten men, one groaned and screamed, "My poor wife! My poor children! What will they do?" Suddenly the frail priest presented himself before the officers, "I would like to die in place of that man."

Colson elaborated,

Kolbe wasn't looking for gratitude. If he was to lay down his life for another, the fulfillment had to be in the act of obedience itself. The joy must be found in submitting his small will to the will of One more grand.

In the basement the ten men were herded into a dark, windowless cell . . . . As the hours and days passed the camp became aware of something extraordinary happening in the death cell. Past prisoners had spent their dying days howling, attacking one another, clawing the walls in a frenzy of despair.

But now, coming from the death box, those outside heard the faint sounds of singing. For this time the prisoners had a shepherd to gently lead them through the shadows of the valley of death, pointing them to the Great Shepherd. And perhaps for that reason Father Kolbe was the last to die.

Two weeks later there were four prisoners still alive in the bunker, but it was needed for more prisoners. So a German doctor went in with a syringe to kill them. "When they swung the bunker door open, there, in the light of their flashlight, they saw Father Maximilian Kolbe, a living skeleton, propped against one wall. His head was inclined a bit to the left. He had the ghost of a smile on his lips and his eyes wide open, fixed on some faraway vision." In a moment, with the drug, he too was dead.

Colson ended this story with these comments, "What went through Maximilian Kolbe's mind when he volunteered to lay down his life for prisoner #5659? No one knows, but the decision was instantaneous, the natural consequence of a character shaped by a lifelong commitment to Christ. What he did resulted from who he was."[10]

What a beautiful and sad story of grace. Author David Seamands stated: "If the ultimate cure is grace, then the ultimate cause of the [performance-oriented] behavior is the failure to understand, experience and live out grace at every level of our lives. Until we do this we are doomed to be Christian POWs. Prisoners of War? No. Prisoners of Works."[11]

Even though Father Kolbe was imprisoned in Auschwitz, he was not a prisoner. For in his spirit, where it truly counts, he was *free*.

Until we know God's grace, we cannot experience the freedom He offers us. We cannot know the freedom recorded in this hymn by Charles Wesley:

My chains fell off!
My heart was free!
I rose, went forth, and followed Thee.
Amazing love!
How can it be
That Thou, My God, shouldst die for me?

◆

Amazing Applications

1. "It is for freedom that Christ has set us free. Stand firm, then, and do not let yourselves be burdened again by a yoke of slavery" (Gal. 5:1). What does the word "freedom" mean to you? What changes would need to happen in your life for you to experience that kind of freedom?

2. Set aside some time to be quiet and reflect on the burden you might be carrying. Picture it as a backpack. Imagine each item that needs to be taken out of the pack in order to lighten your load. What are they? Can you really get rid of those burdens? Can you actually toss them aside and be free? It can only happen with the Lord's help and grace. Take time to thank Him in prayer for what He has done to secure your freedom.

3. Look up these verses and find out what Scripture tells us to do with our burdens: Matthew 11:28–29; Philippians 4:6–7; and 1 Peter 5:7. Each of these would be an excellent promise to commit to memory. Next time you feel the weight of fear or guilt or shame, repeat to yourself one of these verses. Then do what God's Word says!

4. Are you a fearful person? Do you know why? Ask yourself, "What do I fear? Why am I afraid? What previous experiences cause my fear? How would Jesus

embrace this aspect of life?" Psychologist Frank Farley recommends that once you unfold your fear, look for opportunities to triumph over it. For me, letting go of control was very fearful. That's why forcing myself to rappel down mountains helped me learn to trust and let go. In addition, there's no better classroom for being forced to let go of control than to get married and have four kids! What do you need to do?

◆

Grace Memory Verse

Sin shall not be your master,
because you are not under law, but under *grace*.
—Romans 6:14—

◆

CHAPTER EIGHT

Attracted to Godliness

at·'tract·ed *vb:* fascinated by and drawn to emotionally

*T*here was excitement that night in the women's dorm parlor as college students trickled in, finding seats on the couches and floor. Everyone wore jeans and all the gals had long straight hair. Many of the guys did too! It was 1971 and we were in the middle of the "Jesus Movement." Young people everywhere were discovering spiritual truth and our Sunday evening gathering, "College Life," was typical of groups springing up all over the country. I was a freshman at Furman University and had recently committed my life to Christ. Still basking in the joy of newly discovered fellowship and Bible study, I was like an eager sponge ready to soak up Truth.

This particular night we had a special guest speaker. While singing "It only takes a spark . . . ," I looked around in vain for some sign of a dynamic, youthful man, someone who looked like a guest speaker. When the last *"pass it on . . . "* died down, a little old lady walked up to the podium. She looked like someone's grandmother from the Old Country! She wore a frumpy housedress and her white hair was braided in a crown on her head. I was thinking something like, *Give me a break!* But, then, I was only seventeen and hadn't yet learned about the treasure in earthen vessels.

The old lady began to speak with a heavy Dutch accent as she held up a piece of cloth, showing a mass of tangled thread:

My life is but a weaving between my Lord and me,
    I cannot choose the colors, He worketh steadily.
Oftimes He weaveth sorrow, and I, in foolish pride
    Forget He sees the upper and I, the underside.

Turning the cloth over, she revealed a beautiful tapestry picture and continued . . .

Not till the loom is silent and the shuttles cease to fly
    Shall God unroll the canvas and explain the reason why
The dark threads are as needful in the Weaver's skillful hand
As the threads of gold and silver in the pattern He has planned.

By this time we were all completely spellbound!

"My name is Corrie ten Boom and I have spent my life as a tramp for the Lord, telling people all over the world that there is no pit so deep that God is not there! Let me tell you my story . . . " and she began to speak to a hushed and attentive audience.

Tante Corrie, who had just come to the United States to speak at a Billy Graham crusade, went on to tell us about growing up in Holland and hiding Jews in her home during World War II. She described how her family was caught by the Nazis and sent to the Ravensbruck concentration camp. We heard about Betsie, her sister who had died there. We heard about the atrocities of the Holocaust. And we heard about God's presence in that deep pit of Hell.

Tante Corrie *radiated* God's love and compassion. How could I have possibly thought her frumpy? *She was beautiful!* When the evening was over, I thought, *I want what Tante Corrie has. I want to be a godly, courageous, confident woman!*

In the years since, I have read all of Tante Corrie's books, seen *The Hiding Place* movie, and continue to quote her often. But I have never forgotten that night twenty-five years ago when I was first attracted to godliness.

The words *godly* and *godliness* actually appear only a few times in the New Testament; yet the entire Bible is a book on godliness. Jerry Bridges says, "When Paul wants to distill the essence of the Christian life into one brief paragraph, he focuses on godliness. He tells us that God's grace 'teaches us to say No to *ungodliness* and worldly passions, and to live self-controlled, upright and *godly* lives' (Titus 2:11–13) as we await the coming of our Lord Jesus Christ."[1]

Becoming godly is more than just checking off a list each day: served Christ, had devotions, prayed for the world, read my Bible, etc. The basis of godliness is a longing, a thirst for God—"As the deer pants for streams of water, so my soul pants for you, O God. My soul thirsts for God, for the living God" (Ps. 42:1–2a).

Unfortunately, I've had moments in my life when, rather than thirsting for God, I barely made room for Him in my busy schedule!

The Holy Spirit's work of transforming us more and more into the likeness of Christ is called sanctification. In his new book *The Disciplines of Grace*, Jerry Bridges points out that the pursuit of holiness must be anchored in the grace of God; otherwise it is doomed to failure. He says, "Sanctification is the work of the Holy Spirit in us whereby our inner being is progressively changed, freeing us more and more from sinful traits and developing within us over time the virtues of Christlike character. However, though sanctification is the work of the Holy Spirit in us, it does involve our whole-hearted response in obedience and the regular use of the spiritual disciplines that are instruments of sanctification."[2]

Many people find it easier to *do* than to *become*. My friend Susan calls them human *doings*, not human *beings*. One example is those Christians who look toward the fruit of the Spirit as a barometer for godliness: "The fruit of the Spirit is love, joy, peace, patience, kindness, goodness, faithfulness, gentleness and self-control" (Gal. 5:22–23).

Every time I studied those verses I'd make a prayer list: 1. Dear Lord, help me to be more *patient*; 2. Dear Lord, strengthen my *self-control*; 3. Dear Lord, give me *peace* in this situation; and so forth. And then I would try hard to make the prayer be answered by devising a strategy guaranteed to produce the fruit. And, of course, I failed.

One day in my prayer time the Holy Spirit revealed to me that I was going about this the wrong way. My job was not to seek the *fruit* of the Spirit—my job was to seek *Christ*. The fruit would then appear as a natural by-product of a life wholly committed to growing in the likeness of my Lord and Savior.

Once again, friends from a children's book helped show me the way—this time it was *Frog and Toad*. In Arnold Lobel's story "The Garden" Toad decides that he likes Frog's garden and wants to have one too. So he plants some seeds, puts his head close to the ground and yells loudly, "Now seeds, start growing!" Of course, when he looks, it doesn't appear that the seeds are growing.

Frog comes along and encourages Toad to be patient: "Leave them alone for a few days. Let the sun shine on them, let the rain fall on them. Soon your seeds will start to grow."

But Toad is convinced that his seeds are afraid of the dark so he stays up all night reading, singing, and playing music for his seeds. Still they do not appear to grow. Exhausted and disillusioned, he falls asleep.

"Toad, Toad, wake up," says Frog. "Look at your garden!"

Toad looks at his garden. Little green plants are coming up out of the ground. "At last," shouts Toad, "my seeds have stopped being afraid to grow!"

"And now you will have a nice garden too," says Frog.

"Yes," says Toad, "but you were right, Frog. It was very hard work."[3]

Like Toad I have tried to cajole my way into godliness. Impatient with my own spiritual growth, I practically shout, "Now, Cindy, start growing!" But God has shown me that it takes a combination of planting the right seeds in fertile soil plus resting in His love and care to produce fruit that will last.

Out with the how-to books and strategies for becoming holy. *In* with the intentional desire to know Christ better. I worshiped Him. I prayed to Him. I listened in silence. I read His Word. And you know what? The fruit came. Mind you, it came gradually. But Christ's promises to me (and to you too) are true! "I chose you . . . to go and bear fruit—fruit that will last!" (John 15:16).

How perfectly Galatians 5 ties in with John 15: "Remain in me, and I will remain in you. No branch can bear fruit by itself; it must remain in the vine. Neither can you bear fruit unless you remain in me" (John 15:4). So part of desiring godliness is in order that our Father be glorified when, as a result of our seeking the True Vine, we bear much fruit (see John 15:8).

When I first went off to college Mama gave me Hannah Whitall Smith's classic volume *The Christian's Secret of a Happy Life.* It is a well-worn favorite which I have referred to over and over again even though it was first published more than one hundred years ago. About ten years ago I read a new biography about the author and discovered some amazing things.

Hannah Whitall Smith originally wrote that book as installments in her evangelist husband's newsletter; she had agreed to write them if he'd agree not to drink. In addition to being an alcoholic, he had three nervous breakdowns and many publicized affairs before he finally left the faith. Four of Hannah's children died before adulthood. The three remaining children never accepted Christ: Mary deserted her two- and four-year-old daughters to run off to Europe with an artist; Alys married well-known atheist Bertrand Russell and had a nervous breakdown; and Logan became a manic-depressive.

How could Hannah continue to grow in godliness so that she wrote in one of her journals, "Amid many deep and perplexing trials I feel that it is an especial blessing that my faith is not suffered to fail"?

Perhaps it was because she had pursued godliness and developed her inward life. In her book, I underlined these words about what results from a faithful following of the Lord in a consecrated soul:

> Meekness and quietness of spirit become in time the characteristics of the daily life. A submissive acceptance of the will of God, as it comes in the hourly events of each day, is manifested; pliability in the hands of God to do or to suffer all the good pleasures of His will; sweetness under

provocation; calmness in the midst of turmoil and bustle; a yielding to the wishes of others, and an insensibility to slights and affronts; absence of worry or anxiety; deliverance from care and fear—all these, and many other similar graces, are invariably found to be the natural outward development of that inward life which is hid with Christ in God.[4]

I'll bet she needed them too!

In addition to pursuing the inner life, we must pay attention to our relationships with others, for truly that is the testing ground of our practical theology. Author Karen Mains suggests that if we are to be connected to one another in significant ways, we must pursue three courses of action simultaneously: "We must seek to know God, we must seek to know ourselves and we must seek to know both God and ourselves in the company of others.

"My encounters with strangers have shattered my individualistic notion that I could find my own way into God alone. My spiritual journey cannot be a solo crossing. Unaided, I am frighteningly unable to know myself. Any self-sufficiency, any comfort in my own ideas, estranges me from the very Christ I seek to find."[5]

Of course, one of the best ways to learn about godliness is to observe it in the lives of those around us, remembering that we are all "works in progress." I think of a few women and men who have challenged my own pursuit of the holy life:

Evelyn Pratt Secrest—my own paternal grandmother. With a twinkle in her eye, her love for Jesus was contagious to all—whether it be the "fallen women" at her weekly Bible study in the Atlanta jail or the proper Presbyterian Ladies Circle in Decatur. From her I learned that Jesus loves a healthy sense of *humor*. How grateful I am that she passed this on to my daddy, *Pratt Secrest*.

J. Christy Wilson Jr.—my faculty advisor at Gordon-Conwell Seminary. What a man of prayer and vision! From him I learned the importance of *intercessory prayer*: to pray immediately when someone gives a request (even if you're driving a car or in the middle of a public place); to pray for the world and unreached people (always have a world map on your wall, touch each country, and claim it for Christ); and to pray through names of those I don't know as well as loved ones (in seminary it was the student directory, now I pray specifically for each participant whenever I speak to a group).

Ingrid Trobisch—founder of Family Life Mission and pioneer in women's ministry. As her daughter Katrine once told me, "My mother knows how to pour out joy and beauty into hungry souls." Once in India a man approached Ingrid and said, "You are different from any Western woman I've seen and I've finally figured it out. You have something most Western women do not have—serenity." From Ingrid I learned about *serenity*, which comes from the German word *sovereinitat*, meaning "to rise above a situation."

Grace Morgan—former director of Caring Ministries and senior minister's wife at my church. From Grace (who most certainly lives up to her name!) I learned the importance of availability, humility, a servant's spirit, and most of all, *mercy*.

Robert Boyd Munger—a minister/mentor for me in my first pastoral staff position. He has spent his whole life encouraging and discipling young men and women to go forth into the world and make a difference. From him I learned how to truly make Christ "at home in my heart" so that I might *pour myself out for the next generation.*

Ruth Bell Graham—wife of evangelist Billy Graham and once my neighbor in Montreat. As her daughter Anne told me, "What my mother has taught me is that God is enough—period. I have seen her cling to God's promises and presence when she had nothing else and when she had everything else." From her I learned that love involves *sacrifice and letting go.*

David M. Howard—my boss when I worked in Pattaya, Thailand, for the 1980 Consultation on World Evangelization. He has a way of making everyone feel special and an integral part of the team. From him I learned that *friendliness and hope* are important qualities in a Christian leader.

Sarah Hasty Secrest—my mama. From her I learned that there is no more important privilege in life than to be a *prayerful mother.*

Gail MacDonald—author, speaker, and minister's wife who has crossed my path many times over the years. From her I learned that *encouragement*—through spoken affirmations, written notes, and remembering names—is a ministry worth cultivating. Her daughter Kristen says her mom "empties herself so that others might be filled."

Elisabeth Elliot—author and speaker who became a spiritual mother to me long ago. No matter what problem I brought to her, I knew her answer would always take me to the Word of God. From her I learned about *obedience* and *offering our gifts back to God* to use as He chooses. Almost twenty years ago she told a young southern gal who struggled with her theology thesis, "Cindy, God has given you a gift of writing—it is your duty to use it for Him."

Who has been for you an example of godliness? Mine is certainly not an exhaustive list, but it's a start! My apologies to the above folk who, I'm sure, realize that I have not yet mastered the lessons I claim to have learned from them. Nonetheless, something of value did stick and I'm on my way!

So how does grace fit in with godliness? In the book *Pastors at Risk*, Jerry Bridges is quoted as saying, "Anyone who seriously pursues holiness must come to grips with the grace of God. Without an emphasis on grace, we lapse into a performance relationship with God. Then our relationship with Him is gauged on how well we have been doing in pursuing holiness rather than depending on the provisions of Christ. The reality is that many believers do not fully enjoy living in God's grace so it has a transforming effect on their character."[6]

Even though there is no formula for holiness, there are some basics which tend to characterize those bent on conforming to the likeness of Christ.

First, *time with the Lord* is essential. I wake up thanking God for the gifts of life and a new day. I try to live in partnership with Christ by asking Jesus, "What shall we do about this situation today?" or "Will You go with me to that staff meeting today and give me the words to say?"

Second, I know God also reveals His way through *Scripture*. Whether I'm deeply into an inductive study of the Book of 1 Peter; reading my Old Testament/New Testament/Psalm/Proverb selections for the day; or just soaking up the *Daily Light* passages, I know how important it is to focus on some portion of God's Word each day. Though I have read through the entire Bible, each time I re-read a passage it means something fresh and new to me.

Third, in my *personal prayer time* I use an acronym, TRIP, as a guide.

T—*Thanks*: "What do I have to give thanks for?"

R—*Repentance*: "What am I sorry about and need to confess?"

I—*Intercession:* "Whom will I pray for today?" (I use a list.)

P—*Petition:* "What do I need from the Lord today, and what is His plan and purpose for me today?"

This is a good start, but I have also learned to pray throughout the day. When I read the newspaper, I often stop to pray for world situations or the families of crime victims. When I receive requests over our church telephone prayer chain, I stop immediately to take them before the throne of grace. I mail each birthday card or thank-you note off with a prayer for that person. I and my children stop whatever we are doing when we hear a siren and pray for whomever is in trouble and those going to help. (Now that my son serves in emergency rescue and fire-fighting, I'm doubly glad we cultivated this habit—perhaps some mom down in Tennessee is praying for *his* siren.) And I pray briefly with each child and my husband as they leave for the day. Almost every time my college son calls home I also say a short prayer with him on the phone.

Richard Foster calls this "praying the ordinary":

♦ turn ordinary experiences of life into prayer

♦ see God in the ordinary experiences of life

♦ pray throughout the ordinary experiences of life.

He believes that if we cannot find God in the routines of home and shop, then we will not find Him at all.[7]

In addition to such "arrow" prayers, I find that utilizing other's prayers is also quite helpful, particularly John Baillie's *Diary of Private Prayer* which I inherited from my Grandfather Secrest. Also, in *Disciplines of Grace*, Kent Hughes suggests we pray every day through the Ten Commandments. He calls them the "Ten Words of Grace":

> Gracious Lord, enable me to so live that nothing comes before You. Cleanse my life of all idols, material and mental. Help me, God, to never misuse Your holy name. May the Sabbath's genesis rhythm order my spiritual life. Empower me to honor my parents through obedience and reverence. Save me from the anger and hatred of a homicidal heart. Deliver me from the sensuality of an adulterous heart. May I never steal anything. Empower me to be truthful. Mighty God, liberate me from covetousness.[8]

Nothing encourages holiness so much as to study the lives of the great saints of the church. Teresa of Avila, born in 1515, was declared a doctor of the church because of her reform efforts, the profundity of her writings about the spiritual life, and her dynamic faith and love. With her ability to combine common sense and deep mysticism, Teresa showed us what it means to be people alive in our own culture who enter into the depths of our own life and heart and find God there.

One of Teresa's best-known images for spiritual transformation is that of the silkworm at its birth, in its active caterpillar stage, in its cocoon form, and in its butterfly stage. Rosemary Broughton's book, *Praying with Teresa of Avila*, states: "With the silkworm image, Teresa affirms the identity of the soul in the hand of God, the vast differences of each stage of spiritual growth, and the change of form that takes place."

In her book, *Interior Castle,* Teresa wrote her fellow sisters, "Take careful note, daughters, that it is necessary for the silkworm to die, and, moreover, at a cost to your-selves. In the delightful union, the experience of seeing oneself in so new a life greatly helps one to die. . . . This union with God's will is the union I have desired all my life; it is the union I ask the Lord for always and the one that is clearest and safest."

Teresa wanted others to understand that the soul's life with God follows stages. "One of the traits of humility is to recognize and live in the stage that is true to us and to do the work that is given to us to do. The caterpillar cannot fly; it eats. The butterfly no longer creeps; it need not spin silk." Teresa helped me to recognize that there are differing possibilities in each stage.[9]

The hymn writer Thomas Kelly puts it this way in "Praise the Savior, Ye Who Know Him":

> Then we shall be where we would be,
> Then we shall be what we should be;
> Things that are not now, nor could be,
> Soon shall be our own.

Our full sanctification will not be realized this side of heaven, but we can go forth one step at a time. For two years I spent more time with people who couldn't see me than with people who could. Now that's a great opportu-nity to develop that important part of us that's invisible to the eye! I worked twenty counties in western North Caro-lina as a teacher for the blind. During my three months of training, I was blindfolded each day with a black sleepshade and taught how to do everything I would later teach my own visually handicapped clients.

One day I remember tapping my white cane in front of me when a nearby car's horn startled me. Then a dog barked. *Is it restrained?* I wondered. Such fears are common among those who cannot see. My cane "told" me the sidewalk had become uneven as I precariously made my way toward my destination—the Hot Shot Cafe.

My instructor, Bette, had mentioned there was construction on this route, but she also assured me that my cane would "warn" me in time to avert potholes and newly-dug ditches. "Just take it one step at a time," she hollered. "Your cane technique will give you the view a few steps ahead. The rest will be made clear as you go."

But I wanted to know *now* what and where the obstacles were! So I strained my other senses and tried to remember all my orientation and mobility training. I was reconciled to the fact that all I needed to know would be revealed in time, but for now a few steps was all the forewarning I had.

That morning I had been praying for God's guidance concerning possible grad school as well as the future of a romantic relationship. I had also recently memorized: "I will instruct you and teach you in the way you should go; I will counsel you and watch over you" (Ps. 32:8) and "Whether you turn to the right or to the left, your ears will hear a voice behind you, saying, 'This is the way; walk in it'" (Isa. 30:21).

In reflecting on God's promises I knew that God would let me know His way. All I had to do was proceed one step at a time. Just as my cane would reveal the path and give me clues for reaching my destination safely, so God's guidance would do the same for my future.

After completing my training, I worked for the North Carolina Division of Services for the Blind for two years. I never did marry that guy, but I did enroll in graduate school to prepare for ministry. Upon arrival, my faculty advisor gave each new student a scriptural promise to claim for the year. Mine? These clear and prophetic words: "I will lead the blind by ways they have not known, along unfamiliar paths I will guide them; I will turn the darkness into light before them and make the rough places smooth. These are the things I will do; I will not forsake them" (Isa. 42:16).

Quite often new believers will ask me, "But how can I know that it's God who is guiding me and not my own desires?" I believe as we get to know Christ personally and grow in godly character, we will develop a discernment of spiritual truth. His way will become clear, and it will be the only way that gives us true peace inside.

I am attracted to godliness, not because it makes me better, but because it makes me a totally new person. The butterfly looks absolutely nothing like the silkworm it once was. It's not just a better silkworm; it's a totally new creature. And mere improvement is not redemption, even though most certainly those who are born again are improved through sanctification.

But, as C. S. Lewis points out, godliness doesn't just change us; it *transforms* us: "God became man to turn creatures into sons: not simply to produce better men of the old kind but to produce a new kind of man. It is not like teaching a horse to jump better and better but like turning a horse into a winged creature. Of course, once it has got its wings, it will soar over fences which could never have been jumped and thus beat the natural horse at its own game. But there may be a period, while the wings are just beginning to grow, when it cannot do so: and at that stage the lumps on the shoulders—no one could tell by looking at them that they are going to be wings—may even give it an awkward appearance."[10]

Wings, eh? Come fly with me!

◆

Amazing Applications

1. When Betty Scott was a student at Moody Bible Institute she wrote a prayer, committing her life to Christ.

By the early 1940s she and her husband, John Stam, were missionaries to China. When the Communist Red Guard went on a rampage killing "foreign devils," both Betty and John were beheaded, though their baby daughter, Priscilla, survived by being hidden in a barn by Chinese Christians. When I was twenty-three years old I prayed Betty Scott Stam's prayer which has challenged many to pursue the godly life. Perhaps you would like to do the same.

> *Lord, I give up all my own plans and purposes, all my own desires and hopes, and accept Thy will for my life. I give myself, my life, my all utterly to Thee to be Thine forever. Fill me and seal me with Thy Holy Spirit. Use me as Thou wilt, send me where Thou wilt, work out Thy whole will in my life at any cost, now and forever.*

2. The entire chapter of Colossians 3 is full of how we are to seek after godliness by putting on our new self. Read the chapter in your own Bible and make a list of all that God commands (i.e., "set your heart on things above," "put to death sexual immorality," "put to death impurity," etc.). Pray through this list, asking God to help you reflect His image more and more each day.

3. Do you spend time alone with God each day? Whether you call it "quiet time," "devotions," or something else entirely, it is essential! Start by taking a few minutes each day—you'll soon make it longer and longer! Morning is usually the best, but God will meet you anywhere at any time. Try using the acronym TRIP to help guide your prayers.

4. Consider finding an older person of your same sex who has a mature relationship with Jesus Christ. Ask this

person to prayerfully consider being your "mentor" or "spiritual director." Meet with her/him regularly and share what God is teaching you. Having someone to ask the hard questions and hold you accountable for spiritual growth is important. If you can't find a person to do this, read more about those in the past who exercised spiritual disciplines, such as Teresa of Avila.

◆

Grace Memory Verse

Now I commit you to God and to the word of his *grace*, which can build you up and give you an inheritance among all those who are sanctified.

—Acts 20:32—

◆

CHAPTER NINE

Assured of Love

as·'sured *vb:* made certain or given confidence

One snowy January afternoon in Connecticut, I was frantically putting the finishing touches on a conference talk I would be giving the following week. The words were flowing when suddenly I thought that four-year-old Maggie had cooperated beautifully by staying so quiet during her nap time. Of course, right then I heard a meek little voice, "Mama, I have something to tell you."

"What is it, hon?" I absentmindedly queried while closing my notebook and looking around to see the little person who went with the voice.

Just then she slowly peered from around the door and exclaimed, "Mama, I cut off all my hair!"

And she had.

Her shoulder-length pageboy had been turned into a punk-like butch with several bangs only one-eighth inch long! For once in my life, I was totally speechless. But in those first few seconds I heard a very clear voice inside my head, "Careful, Cindy! She will *always* remember the way you handle this one!" After studying about grace for so long, I was suddenly faced with the lab exam!

So instead of my usual dramatic overreaction, I simply pulled her close for comfort and a hug. Maggie knew that what she had done was wrong, and she already showed signs of regret: "Mama, can you make my hair long again? Mama, am I still pretty? Mama, do you still love me?"

With her words I decided to forego my actions-have-consequences sermon and just wash her hair (she had also "moussed" it up with hand cream), trim it neatly and tell her that no matter what she did or what she looked like, I would always love her. For her, at that time, it was enough.

How often have I blown it big time and shuffled into the presence of God saying, "Lord, I have something to tell you . . . "? I come not only for confession but also to find assurance.

Does God thunder out His condemnation of me, "You jerk! I can't believe you did that again for the 139th time! Will you never learn? I'm outta here . . . !"

Hardly. Instead, I do what Ingrid Trobisch once suggested to me. I figuratively crawl up into the lap of my heavenly Father and *let myself be loved.*

Do you remember when you had your first theology lesson on love? If you're like me, it was probably at about one year old. The reason I remember mine is thanks to the modern technology of reel-to-reel tape recorders in 1954 on which my Daddy recorded such early apologetics. As I listen to the tape of my adorable toddler voice, I realize I learned my lesson pretty well: "Jesus loves me, this I know. For the . . . for the . . . for the . . . (What for, Daddy? Oh yeah . . .) For the Bible tells me so. Little ones to Him belong. They are weak, but He is strong. Yes, Jesus loves

me. Yes, Jesus loves me. Yes, Jesus loves me. For the Bible
tells me so."

If so many of us started out learning such marvelous
truth about God's love, why, then, do we still fail to grasp
the reality of it? Don't just teach your children to sing
"Jesus Loves Me"; teach them to believe it by believing it
yourself!

One godly man put it this way: "Christianity is not
primarily a moral code, but a grace-laden mystery; it is not
essentially a philosophy of love, but a love affair; it is not
keeping rules with clenched fists, but receiving a gift with
open hands."[1]

Are you having a love affair with Jesus? Or is your
Christian life better described as a "philosophy of love"? I
was twenty-three years old when I first fell in love. He was
a young camp director named Paul, and I most certainly
thought this was *it!* I wanted to be with Paul all the time
and when I wasn't, I thought about him or wrote letters to
him or created gifts and surprises to communicate how
special I thought he was.

This same fervor should characterize our relationship
with Christ, who initiated a great love for us. But too often
we are disappointed in love, as I eventually was with Paul.
Something goes wrong and we are left feeling discarded
and unworthy. Somehow we subconsciously expect God's
love to be like human love—contingent on any number of
human variables. But it's not!

The apostle Paul graphically reminds us of this truth:
"Do you think anyone is going to be able to drive a wedge
between us and Christ's love for us? There is no way! Not
trouble, not hard times, not hatred, not hunger, not home-
lessness, not bullying threats, not backstabbing, not even
the worst sins listed in scripture. . . . None of this fazes us
because Jesus loves us. I'm absolutely convinced that nothing—nothing living or dead, angelic or demonic, today or

tomorrow, high or low, thinkable or unthinkable— absolutely nothing can get between us and God's love because of the way that Jesus our Master has embraced us" (Rom. 8:35–39, *The Message*).

In his book, *The Ragamuffin Gospel*, Brennan Manning reminds us that ragamuffins (the bedraggled, beat up, and burnt out) must never forget that the love of Jesus Christ is stronger than death and endures forever. "Everything else will pass away, but the love of Christ is the same yesterday, today and forever. In the end, it is the one thing you can hang onto!"[2]

Earlier in Romans 8 Paul tells us that all our struggles can't possibly compare with all Christ has in store for us when He returns: "I consider that our present sufferings are not worth comparing with the glory that will be revealed in us" (Rom. 8:18).

Seminary president Brian Chapell elaborates, "The words remind us that if God loved us enough to sacrifice his Son to save us in the past, and if we will experience the riches of his love in the future, then God must also love us in the time between, even if it holds some difficulty. Through his apostle God says to each of us, 'If I love you at the beginning of our journey and promise to love you when we reach our destination, then there is no reason to doubt my love along the way, even if the road gets bumpy.'"[3]

I met my friend Glenda in the lobby of the Philadelphia Airport Marriott. She was the only other person in the lobby who wasn't part of the Los Angeles Rams football team so we naturally "discovered" each other. We were both waiting for a shuttle to take us to a retreat center in Maryland where our lives would soon be changed forever through a new understanding of grace. Among other things, Glenda gave me a marvelous tool that her Bible study in Georgia used. To better understand God's unconditional love for them, each day they were encouraged to repeat this phrase, "I have great value apart from my performance because Christ gave His life for me, and therefore imparted great value to me. I am deeply loved, fully pleasing, totally forgiven, accepted and complete in Christ." Now I have that same phrase written on a 3 x 5 card and hope that if I repeat it enough I'll eventually come to believe it!

What assures you of love? My oldest daughter is named Fiona, which is the Gaelic word for "fair one." As beautiful inside as she is outside, Fiona was cared for during the first two months of her life by dear friends of her parents. That's because her birth mother discovered she had liver cancer at Fiona's birth. During that first year of this little girl's life her Mommy Inka was often in too much pain to hold her close. Fortunately, her dad and many others loved her dearly and were there for her when her mom died.

I was overjoyed to have Fiona as my little girl! I'll never forget the first time I met her—a petite three-year-old in a navy blue coat standing sheepishly with her daddy at the airport gate. In my naturally effusive way, I showered her with love, hugs, and all kinds of assurances that I was going to be around for the long haul. During her preschool years it became a custom for me to put her to bed with the little song, "I love you, a bushel and a peck . . ." Somehow this silly little song seemed to comfort her with my love.

One day we had just returned from playgroup where she had watched *Charlotte's Web* on video. After putting Fiona down for a nap, I heard the sound of soft crying.

"What's wrong, honey?" I gently asked, entering her room.

"The . . . spider . . . died . . . !" she sobbed with uncharacteristic emotion. Somehow that story by E. B. White had broken through and enabled her to finally grieve her losses. For a long time she cried, and I held her close. She wanted to know all about death and heaven. She wanted to know if she'd have *two* mommies there.

And she wanted to know if she'd be there too. It was a *kairos* (an inbreak of God) moment for us. On her bed, that very day in January 1985, Fiona prayed to receive Christ in her heart and we even made a little plaque to commemorate the occasion. I believe that Christ's love became real to her in a new way that day.

Because God's very nature is LOVE, He cannot be other than what He is. Oh sure, we can refuse the love of God. In fact, most of us have at one point or another in our lives found perfectly good reasons to do just that. But we can never stop God from loving us: "We can reject God's love and thus stop its inflow into us, but we can do nothing to stop its outflow from Him. Grace is the unconditional love of God in Christ freely given to the sinful, the undeserving and the imperfect."[4]

One of my very favorite children's books is *The Runaway Bunny* by Margaret Wise Brown. Written in 1942, it is still a classic for young and old alike. The book is about a little bunny who wants to run away. But no matter how or where he decides to go, his mother is always there—for she loves her little bunny very much.

When the bunny says he'll become a rock on a high mountain, the mother replies that she will then become a mountain climber and climb to where he is. When he decides to hide in a garden as a crocus, she declares that she will become a gardener and find him. And when he threatens to become a bird and fly away from her, she calmly proclaims that she will then become a tree that he comes home to. After several more scenarios the little bunny realizes the relentless love of his mother and decides, "Shucks, I might just as well stay where I am and be your little bunny."[5]

As the mother of four, I certainly identify with the mother bunny. But as a potential "runaway bunny" myself, I also find great comfort in knowing that wherever I may flee, God, the great "Hound of Heaven," will be there for me.

King David knew about God's continuous presence and love. I guess he learned the hard way, but it did get through by the time he penned Psalm 139: "O LORD, you have searched me and you know me . . . You have laid your hand upon me. . . . Where can I go from your Spirit? Where can I flee from your presence? If I go up to the heavens, you are there; if I make my bed in the depths you are there. If I rise on the wings of the dawn, if I settle on the far side of the sea, even there your hand will guide me, your right hand will hold me fast. . . . For you created my inmost being; you knit me together in my mother's womb. I praise you because I am fearfully and wonderfully made. . . . How precious to me are your thoughts, O God! How vast is the sum of them!" (vv. 1, 5, 7–11, 13–14, 17).

One night recently my friend Caroline asked a very good question, "Did Jesus die on the cross for everybody?"

I hardly thought before I blurted out my answer, "Yes, oh yes. Some people will die for good people, but Jesus died for us before we were good (see Rom. 5:6–8). He doesn't ask us to be loving before He loves us. And though our world makes promises based on how well we respond, Christ loves us regardless of our response."

Martin Luther was right. "God does not love us because we are valuable, but we are valuable because God loves us." I guess it all comes down to *grace*—a difficult concept for us because we intrinsically believe we must do something in order to *deserve* Christ's love. But God doesn't want my worth, efforts, gifts, credentials, and produce. He wants me simply because I am me! And if I sit quietly and listen, He assures me of this.

Author Ruth Senter explained it this way:

> If tomorrow you should become anything other than what you are today, still I would want you. If you were in a horrible fire burned beyond recognition, if you contracted a dread disease and became deaf and dumb and if you could not lift a finger to love anymore, still I would want you. My love is for you, not for what you are. . . . So do not strive for perfection. Rather, open yourself to My love. Fix your eyes on the deep wide ocean that cannot contain My love for you. Look to the sky and know that from east to west you will not find the beginning or ending of My love for you. . . . Feel My longing for My absentee Son whom I sent to you, and then you will know how great is My love for you.[6]

My own response? What other response can I give than to consecrate my life to Him? To worship and love and sing with all the strength and power within me, as in the hymn by George Matheson,

> O Love that wilt not let me go,
> I rest my weary soul in Thee,
> I give Thee back the life I owe,
> That in Thine ocean depths its flow
> May richer, fuller be.

Often music gets through to my very soul in a way that other media do not. Knowing that Matheson wrote that hymn after his fiancée left him upon discovering his impending blindness makes the words especially significant to me. A few years ago I heard a song on the Focus on the Family radio program called "Danny's Downs." I didn't even catch the name of the artist, but I was deeply touched as most parents of mentally handicapped children would be upon hearing the hopeful and encouraging lyrics.

Imagine my surprise to discover that the musician, Michael Kelly Blanchard, lived nearby me here in Connecticut. Michael gave a concert at our church on July 4, 1992. Very fitting that it should be called "Independence Day" because I was in the middle of my grace tutorial and that night I was unsuspectingly freed!

It was the first time I heard the song, "I Love You, I Do, You Bet!" The words so penetrated my heart that I have listened to it many times since then.

The song speaks of several people who have made big mistakes. But in each refrain, God emphasizes that there is nothing we've done that is beyond His forgiveness and unconditional love.

Not too long ago, Michael agreed to sing this live as a closing to one of my conference talks in Boston. Just before the last refrain, he stopped and pointed out that these words were from God to all of us with "no exceptions!" He's right about God's unconditional love. It is the only thing we can be sure of.

On the twenty-fifth anniversary of the Auca killing of her husband and four other missionaries, Elisabeth Elliot wrote a reflection on those events and the subsequent victories and defeats.

> How we long to point to something—any-thing—and say, "This works! This is sure!" But if it is something other than God Himself we are destined for disappointment. There is only one ultimate guarantee. It is the love of Christ. *The love of Christ.* Nothing in heaven or earth or hell can separate us from that, and because God is God and loves us He will not allow us to rest anywhere but in that Love. We run straight to Him when other

refuges fail. Our misconceptions are corrected in
Him, our failures redeemed, our sins cleansed, our
griefs turned to joy. But first "the life also of Jesus
must be manifest in our mortal bodies." First the
drama must be played out—through suffering,
weakness, failure, death, and resurrection.[7]

I have seen the face of Love, and it truly is the face of
my Lord and Savior, Jesus Christ.

◆

Amazing Applications

1. What does love really look like? The Bible gives us
   many examples, but my two favorite ones are 1 Corinthians 13 and Romans 12:9–21. Look up these passages
   and list the manifestations of love. If you don't recognize many in yourself, perhaps you need a new view of
   God's love for you. Why not try defining yourself as
   "one loved by God" or "the Beloved."

2. Do you truly believe that there is nothing you can do
   to earn God's love and nothing you can do to lose God's
   love? Believe it! Psalm 118 is entirely devoted to pre-
   senting God's unchanging love in the midst of chang-
   ing situations. If you need more confidence in God's
   love for you, take time to read this psalm and underline
   every promise of God's unfailing love. I believe the
   most important message I can help communicate to
   others is how much God loves us. I hope you have a
   greater understanding after reading this chapter and
   the promises from God's Word.

3. Sometimes grace looks like discipline, and sometimes
   grace looks like love. When Maggie cut her hair, I
   somehow sensed that in her fragile state I was to
   reassure her of my love. The discipline part would have
   to come later. Unfortunately, there have been too many

times when, caught by surprise, I've reacted instead of prayerfully asking God to show me how to act. I'll bet you have too. Why not take some time now to ask God's forgiveness for your unloving ways?

4. Have you, like Runaway Bunny, tested God to see how far you could go (or how bad you could be) before He let go of His love? Does Psalm 139 assure you that "even if you make your bed in hell" (as one translation says) God will be there? Some have done that very thing—thank God that He is truly there when we hit rock bottom.

◆

Grace Memory Verse

May our Lord Jesus Christ himself and God our Father, who loved us and by his *grace* gave us eternal encouragement and good hope, encourage your hearts and strengthen you in every good deed and word.

—2 Thessalonians 2:16–17—

◆

CHAPTER TEN

Anointed to Serve

a·'noint·ed *vb*: consecrated

*M*y 1968 Ford rattled across the bridge deep in the hollows of Kentucky. For the first time in my life, I fully appreciated the term "with a wing and a prayer," for I literally prayed for angels' wings to carry me across that rickety bridge each day. Rounding the bend I caught sight of the Cadwells' place (actually, the scent hit me before the sight).

The old, weathered house stood on a hill. On the porch and throughout the yard were piles and piles of old clothes that well-meaning people had donated to the family. Unfortunately, no one had bothered to sort through them—a task which bewildered the Cadwells. And so the piles just sat there—crumpled, wet, and moldy.

As I arrived, Jim, a handsome tow-headed boy of ten, ran down to greet "Miss Cindy." Every day I took him to the nearby hollow where I directed a recreation and enrichment program for the mountain children. Jim was beautiful and bright—a ray of hope among the squalor. He lived with his mother, aunt, and uncle—all mentally retarded. Standing tall on the porch, they certainly made a formidable trio, but either I was too idealistic to be concerned or I was just plain young and foolish.

Either way, in that summer of 1973 while the rest of the world stayed glued to Watergate on TV (I'm kind of relieved to have missed that chapter of history), I traipsed around Kentucky wearing cutoff overalls and long braids, feeling quite invincible. *Surely if I am serving others in Jesus' name, He won't let any harm come to me!* I thought. So . . . what was a nice young coed like me doing in a place like this?

By the time I was nineteen years old, I had read Catherine Marshall's fictional tribute to her mother, *Christy*, at least three times. I now had a heroine and I wanted to be just like Christy—to serve the rural poor with Christ's love, to bring them hope, to change the world! And so, just after my twentieth birthday, I set off to serve on summer staff with Christian missions in the mountains of Kentucky.

I lived in a "holler" with an elderly widow named Miz Beane. There I learned how to quilt, clear fields, wash my hair in rainwater I'd collected in a big tub (we had no running water), use an outhouse, get used to being teased as an "old maid," and eat biscuits three times a day! I was there to *serve*. I thought I'd help these people and give their children something fun to do that summer. I honestly thought I could change their lives. But, in reality, God used this time to change mine.

God's grace stepped in and redeemed my efforts that summer. He took a young, privileged, sheltered college student and opened my eyes to a world of need, softened my heart to hear His voice, and brought me to the end of myself so that I might allow God to work *through* me.

These verses in my Bible were well-underlined, "But we have this treasure in jars of clay to show that this all-surpassing power is from God and not from us" (2 Cor. 4:7). This was the promise I clung to every time I set out to serve God in any way. On my own it would be merely "works." But as I claimed God's power through His Holy Spirit, I was truly anointed to serve. And it wasn't hard at all giving God the glory! Somehow He chose to work through me, not because I was worthy, but because I was willing.

I have said yes to God scores of times since, knowing full well I was not equipped for the task at hand. Still, I believed that "The one who calls you is faithful and he will do it" (1 Thess. 5:24). "Sure, I'll be an editor for a twelve-page, four-language newspaper at a European confer-ence . . . . Sure, I'll write and produce a daily radio news program to be broadcast over seven states. . . . Sure, I'll move to San Francisco even though I know no one west of the Mississippi. . . . Sure, I'll be happy to be a Cub Scout leader. . . . Sure, I'll speak from a flat-bed truck in Malawi, visit refugee camps in Thailand, work at a rescue mission in Boston's Combat Zone, write a book . . . .Yes, yes, *yes!*"

And then always, when the dust settled, *What in the world have I gotten myself into this time?*

Madeleine L'Engle says that we are all asked to do more than we can do. "Every hero and heroine of the Bible does more than he would have thought it possible to do. . . . In a very real sense, not one of us is qualified, but it seems God continually chooses the most unqualified to do His work, to bear His glory. If we are qualified, we tend to think that we have done the job ourselves. If we are forced to accept our evident lack of qualification, then there's no danger that we will confuse God's work with our own or God's glory with our own."[1]

The more I have seen of the world's pain and need, the more I believe Christ has called me to serve as He served—to go on a journey with Him that may include both weary grief and great joy. Sometimes I feel that the ways in which I serve are not terribly life-changing—emptying trash cans, cooking meals, chairing committee meetings, washing laundry, addressing envelopes, driving errands, taking phone messages . . . . But even these daily responsibilities are acts of love when done *"as unto the Lord."*

Irish missionary Amy Carmichael spent fifty-five years in India without a furlough. She rescued hundreds of young children from temple prostitution. She also lived in physical pain most of that time, due to a freak accident. But remarkably enough, she offered her gifts of creative writing back to the Lord. In one of her unusual volumes we read,

> His thoughts said, *My work is not important. Would it matter very much if a floor were left unswept or a room left untidied? Or if I forgot to put flowers for a guest, or omitted some tiny unimportant courtesy?*
>
> His Father said, *Would it have mattered very much if a few people had been left without wine at a feast? But thy Lord turned water into wine for them.*
>
> And the son remembered the words, *Jesus took a towel.*[2] (See John 13:4–5 when Jesus washed the disciples's feet.)

Several years ago, when my husband, Mike, was dean of students at a Christian college, he took a group of students on a summer missions trip to Jamaica. As the plane flew over Montego Bay, Mike had a brief wistful moment in viewing the luxury hotels and sparkling beaches. But soon his crew was driving through Kingston in the worst possible slums. Mike's heart was immediately touched, and he spent the next ten days helping to bring hope into the lives of the poor people of Mandeville.

Every day their team hauled water to mix with concrete in order to build a one-room house. The work was hot, heavy, and hard, but Mike and the college students discovered a whole new joy in working as a team and serving others.

"It was important for me to go to Jamaica because the joy derived from serving the Lord and needy people far outweighed any momentary pleasure I might have experienced lying on a beach in Montego Bay. Plus, I knew we had really made a difference in the lives of at least one homeless family," he later told me.

"One epileptic teenager named John showed up at our work site every day to watch and encourage us. I couldn't help but notice that he needed shoes and appeared to have feet similar to my size. As I left for the airplane flight home, I took off my Reeboks and handed them to John. I will never forget his face . . . ."

That experience stayed with Mike. Even as I write today, my husband, now a minister, is on another missions team—this time in Moscow and St. Petersburg, Russia. But instead of building houses, they are building leadership. Mike and others from our church are training pastors and teachers and, of course, depending on the anointing of the Holy Spirit to accomplish these tasks. I can't wait to hear what God does this time!

Back in 1970, when I recommitted my life to Christ, friends encouraged me to choose a "life verse"—a special promise from God to hold before me for the rest of my life. I honestly don't remember the exact circumstances of how I chose this verse, but I distinctly remember from that point on my "life verse" was Isaiah 58:10–11. My friends were right. It continues to be a rallying cry for each new challenge in my life: "If you spend yourselves on behalf of the hungry and satisfy the needs of the oppressed, then your light will rise in the darkness, and your night will become like the noonday. The Lord will guide you always; he will satisfy your needs in a sun-scorched land and will strengthen your frame. You will be like a well-watered garden, like a spring whose waters never fail."

To serve is to allow ourselves to be channels of Jesus' love and grace—content to be the vessel. Recently I was asked to help plan and carry out the Summit of Christian Women Leaders. Fifty women from all over New England gathered to pray, strategize, and share ministry. I was honored to have been invited, and I was thrilled to be able to meet some of the speakers and Bible teachers I had only heard about since moving to the region.

My very dear friend and prayer partner, Maggie Rowe, was the director of this event through her position as Coordinator of Women's Ministries for the Evangelistic Association of New England. As I thought about the upcoming weekend I was excited in recalling several other venues where Maggie and I had teamed together to speak or emcee. Somehow the chemistry clicked and we made a great team! I thought perhaps this experience might be similar.

But as I prayed through the list of Summit participants, I sensed a clear word from the Lord. "I want you to take the role of a servant this weekend." No up-front presence, no calling-the-shots, simply serving as Maggie's "gofer" and helping the other women in any way necessary. So I began to pray that God would give me a servant's heart.

I arrived at the retreat center early and set up food and drinks for the opening gathering. I had fun carefully choosing healthy fruit and vegetables with dip, hors d'oevres, and seltzer water. I covered tables with colorful linen cloth and placed vases of silk pansies everywhere. It was also a joy to be a greeter, hostess, chair- and table-mover, and early morning coffee maker.

That night I administered first-aid on a cut finger, located Maggie's misplaced briefcase, and even plunged someone's toilet at midnight. At times I had to leave the meeting during a fascinating discussion, but I'd remind myself, *Because I'm taking care of this, it allows someone else to stay and listen.*

When it came right down to it, I wasn't all that great of a servant at the Summit—I interrupted Maggie a few times and probably overlooked some needs. Besides, it was easy helping the same ladies who are usually organizing programs for everyone else. But I learned an important lesson on servant leadership: do it for Jesus, and it will give you joy!

But, of course, we cannot serve very long or effectively in our own strength and that is why God sent the Holy Spirit to dwell in us, to enable us to be Christ's hands to the world. I am often reminded of the English village which was bombed during World War II. In its town square stood a statue of Jesus with outstretched arms atop a pedestal which read "Come unto Me." After the bombing, the townspeople made it a priority to rebuild the statue. But the arms and hands had been utterly destroyed and were nowhere to be found. Instead of replacing them, the townspeople simply engraved on a new pedestal these words, "He has no hands, but our hands."

I often marvel that *we*—sinful, broken humanity—are God's "Plan A" for reaching a world with His love and hope. There is no "Plan B"! If we don't do it, it simply won't happen.

The story is told of Indians in a developing country who regularly walked fifteen miles out of their way to go to the mission hospital.

Perplexed, the Christian doctor asked them, "Why do you do it? The government hospital is closer to you and the medicine is the same. Why don't you just go there?"

The Indians answered, "The medicine is the same, but the hands are different."

The hands that made the difference were hands made gentle by the love of Christ.[3] Truly Christ has no hands but our hands!

About thirteen years ago, I spent a good deal of time training prospective missionaries to cross cultures and be servants to people from vastly different backgrounds. One thing I tried to emphasize was to avoid any semblance of the "ugly American." When we go somewhere as a learner, others begin to value what they have to give. Very few ethnocentric Americans realize just how haughty and superior we appear to those from other cultures. But Catholic priest Henri Nouwen, having spent six months in Peru, knew what it meant to be God's servant.

As I read of his experiences, I began to understand that gratitude is perhaps the central virtue of one who chooses to serve others in the name of Christ. "It is hard for me to accept that the best I can do is probably not to give but to receive. By receiving in a true and open way, those who give to me can become aware of their own gifts. After all, we come to recognize our own gifts in the eyes of those who receive them gratefully."[4]

Now I see a whole new dimension to serving—receiving from others, thereby affirming their gifts. Opportunities abound!

Two years ago, Tim, our high school junior, decided to skip a year and graduate early. I shouldn't have been too shocked since I had made the same choice years before. So he completed his junior and senior studies in one year, received his Eagle Scout, and enrolled at Covenant College at age seventeen. He and I had spent the previous fall driving through the South college-hunting. One beautiful day in the Great Smokey Mountains I decided to treat him to the food he missed the most while living in New England—biscuits and sawmill gravy. No sooner had we settled into a booth at a very promising country cafe than our waitress appeared with a cheerful "Good mornin'! What can I get y'all for breakfast today?"

I don't know if it was her southern accent, friendly smile, bottomless coffee pot, or endless biscuits, but Tim and I melted. For the next hour we basked in her undivided attention as though we had just escaped a Yankee prison and were starved for southern hospitality.

When the bill arrived, it was eight dollars. As Tim finished he said, "Mom, that was the best service we've ever had! I think you should leave her a four-dollar tip."

Now, I'm not particularly stingy, but I wasn't used to tipping 50 percent. Nonetheless, Tim was adamant and he was right. I did want to do something to express our gratitude. I left the four-dollar tip, thus graciously receiving her service as a gift.

The other important lesson I have learned about serving is to do it from my weakness, not my strength. How does one get from a point of pain to the point of being a "wounded healer"? Through the carrying grace of others.

One who vividly offered *carrying grace* to me when we first moved to Connecticut was Grace, my predecessor as director of caring ministry. No sooner had our family of six moved into the parsonage in early December than all of us came down with a terrible flu. All of us! I was too weak to even bathe and feed my two-year-old, much less anyone else.

I knew no one. One person I had met, however, was the senior minister's wife, Grace. But these were people to whom I wanted to show my best side, not my needy side! Nonetheless, my "babies" needed help, so I swallowed my pride and called Grace. She was over with a hot meal and a quiet serving manner in no time at all.

We certainly didn't have a doctor yet, but the husband of someone on Mike's search committee was some kind of doctor, so in desperation we called Will at home. I don't remember much from that night. But I do remember lying in bed, aware that Grace was bathing Maggie in the next room. Will was examining me and I kept apologizing for putting everyone out. "Why?" he said, "Everyone gets sick sometime." After he declared me delirious due to my fever, I promptly threw up.

What a way to start a new pastorate! But what a perfect place and time to come to terms with my own limitations and allow others to serve me. I didn't realize just how deeply this experience had affected me until four years later when I was sharing this story with my Bible study group and started crying.

Author Gail MacDonald knows *carrying grace* first-hand. "Without it we fallen ones would simply remain immobilized where we stumbled. Without it we would eventually turn back and quit climbing. But this carrying grace of God lifts us to our feet and helps us take our first tentative steps forward again. If we, like others who have known pain, are intact today with a heart's desire to serve, it is not because of anything in us. We have simply received grace. We take no credit for it. How can you boast about a gift?"[5]

For those of us who have recognized this grace in our own lives, it seems only natural to offer it back to God, asking how He will use it to touch others. Why are we often surprised at the methods He chooses? Because God's economy is not the same as the world's economy. God says there can be dignity and purpose in every task, beauty in every living part of His creation. The world, on the other hand, exalts fame, power, fortune, titles, and achievement—and degrades those who are not part of the success cycle.

Joni Earekson Tada has spent more than twenty-five years as a quadriplegic, bringing light into the darkness of those who are physically handicapped. Today, through her Joni and Friends Ministries, she partners with other disabled Christians traveling all over the world spreading the love of Christ. Her message is that God doesn't look for people who will fit in or stand out, but for those who will stand up for Him:

> If I were God, I wouldn't do things that way. Had I lived during the time when Israel was voting for a king, I would have served as campaign manager in the political machinery behind Saul—sharp, smooth, fast-talking, good-looking Saul would have made a hit on Jerusalem's version of "Larry King Live." And David, the kid who smelled like sheep? No way. I'd never have bet he'd make it past the primary.
>
> Thank God I'm not running the world. *He* is. And He opens His arms wide not only to kids who tend sheep, but to all the other unlovely and unlikely people. All through the Bible God shows us that this is exactly the way He does things to bring maximum glory to Himself. [6]

My most recent lesson in servanthood (though not my last, I'm sure) has to do with the realization that God wants us to be *willing* more than He wants us to be *able*. Once again, I am helped by Henri Nouwen, who now lives near Toronto at Daybreak, one of the L'Arche communities for mentally handicapped people.

> The first thing that struck me when I came to live in a house with mentally handicapped people

was that their liking or disliking me had absolutely nothing to do with any of the many useful things I had done until then. Since nobody could read my books, they could not impress anyone; and since most of them never went to school, my twenty years at Notre Dame, Yale, and Harvard did not provide a significant introduction. My considerable ecumenical experience proved even less valuable. When I offered some meat to one of the assistants during dinner, one of the handicapped men said to me, "Don't give him meat, he doesn't eat meat, he's a Presbyterian."

Not being able to use any of the skills that had proved practical in the past was a real source of anxiety. I was suddenly faced with my naked self, open for affirmations and rejections, hugs and punches, smiles and tears, all dependent simply on how I was perceived at the moment. In a way, it seemed as though I was starting my life all over again. Relationships, connections, reputations could no longer be counted on.

This experience was and, in many ways, is still the most important experience of my new life, because it forced me to rediscover my true identity. These broken, wounded, and completely unpretentious people forced me to let go of my relevant self—the self that can do things, show things, prove things, build things—and forced me to reclaim that unadorned self in which I am completely vulnerable, open to receive and give love regardless of any accomplishments.[7]

Where to begin? Opportunities to serve others rarely come scheduled neatly in my datebook. They are, by their very nature, interruptions in life. And, unless I have cleared my calendar enough to allow for interruptions, I will probably miss many divine appointments. Easy to say. Hard to do. I feel as though I'm the worst offender in this area. My friends say, "Cindy is the busiest person I know." Every time I hear that, I cringe.

With age and some wisdom, I have learned that a vital part of serving is the discernment to know what I can't do. I call it "selective neglect." I know I can't do it all, so I choose what is expendable. Jill Briscoe calls it learning "the art of leaving things undone" and describes it this way:

> I've found that even though there is a world to be won, God expects me to first attend to the mission field between my own two feet. That's my bit of world and I will certainly be held accountable for it. There are hungry millions to be fed, but God only expects me to offer up the fish and bread in my own lunch basket. There are children to be trained, but I am peculiarly responsible first and foremost to raise my own, in the nurture and admonition of the Lord. And there are certainly lots of Christians to be discipled, counseled, and helped to keep on keeping on, but I didn't save them, and I don't have to keep them! It's all a matter of the art of leaving things undone.[8]

In his devotional book, *My Utmost for His Highest*, Oswald Chambers says, "A Christian is not one who proclaims the Gospel merely, but one who becomes broken bread and poured out wine in the hands of Jesus Christ for other lives."[9]

I was reminded of his words this past weekend at our church's annual women's retreat—this year's theme being "Beauty from Ashes." Our speaker had said that "one way to discover whether or not you are a servant is by how you act when people treat you like one!" Ouch.

God had worked in marvelous ways and so many prayers had been answered in the lives of those special ladies. After a final time of sharing, we closed with a communion service. One of our ministers led the service while I assisted in the sacrament (my first time). We had the 150 women form two lines down the aisle. As they reached the table, Pat and I would dip the bread in a common goblet and say to the individual in front of us, "This is Christ's body and blood given for you."

As the women filed by, I was so struck by the solemnity and beauty of this moment. I looked deep into each one's eyes and said her name. Since most of them were people I knew and had been praying for, I was greatly moved in giving them the bread and cup. I knew there was sorrow, suffering, and pain in those eyes—but I saw joy, gratitude, and hope as well. I had served them through this event and by the time we finished, tears were streaming down my face. I wondered how in the world ministers ever make it through this sacrament dry-eyed!

I think the only way to close this chapter is with the framed words by Mother Teresa which sit on my desk:

We can do no great things for God.
Only small things with great love.

◆

Amazing Applications

1. Acceptable service to God is manifesting His grace by the way we live. To have God's grace and not appropriate it is to have it poured out through the power of the Holy Spirit in vain. Can you think of a time when you wanted to serve Christ but felt totally inadequate? Now you probably realize that at that point of need God wanted through His grace, to anoint you with power to serve Him. Does knowing this make you more eager

to take risks for Him in future endeavors that are clearly His calling? I hope so.

2. In the chapter 3 applications, I suggested you say no to something. In this chapter I suggest you prayerfully say yes to something and claim God's power to work through you as a vessel of His grace. Consider this verse: "And God is able to make all grace abound to you, so that in all things at all times, having all that you need, you will abound in every good work" (2 Cor. 9:8). Don't forget to give Him all the glory!

3. Think of a time when you were at the end of your resources or even at the end of your rope. Did you pray for God to anoint you with His Spirit and give you what you needed to continue to serve? What situation do you face right now that only He can enable you to accomplish? You may just be amazed at what He will accomplish through you, a willing vessel of His love.

4. Gert Behanna, author of *The Late Liz*, discovered an unusual way to serve those she would never meet. Every time she used a public toilet, she would take great care in completely cleaning it until it shone for the next occupant. It was her way of giving to someone who could never thank her. Gert learned that as she did something "unto the least of these" she did it unto Christ. What creative way could you serve someone this week without them ever knowing it was you?

◆

Grace Memory Verse

I became a servant of this gospel by the gift of God's *grace* given me through the working of his power."
—Ephesians 3:7—

◆

CHAPTER ELEVEN

Acquainted with Suffering

ac·'quaint·ed *vb:* having personal knowledge of

I hated housecleaning! But as I dusted this particular New England home, my eyes took in every detail. The living room walls were deep red. I had never seen red walls in my life, but these were beautiful. They set off the furniture and rugs, the needlepointed dining chairs, giving an almost regal touch. Each small detail revealed something about its owner—the delicate china teacups, the well-worn classic books, everything-in-its-place neatness, the piano, and, of course, the six-foot Auca spears propped in the corner!

As a first-year seminarian, I had miraculously stumbled into a lodging situation in the home of author Elisabeth Elliot who had recently been widowed by her second husband, Dr. Addison Leitch. The Auca spears were similar to the ones which had killed her first husband, missionary Jim Elliot, many years before in the jungles of Ecuador.

They had been given to her during the time she and daughter Valerie lived with that same jungle tribe.

As her lodger I was to do some housecleaning, help with airport transportation for her speaking trips, take care of her Scottie, "MacDuff" and do some typing on her current writing project, *The Journals of Jim Elliot*. It was humbling and sobering to type Jim Elliot's own words from his stained jungle diary: "October 29, 1955—First time I ever saw an Auca—fifteen hundred feet is a long way if you're looking out of an airplane. Nate and Ed have found two sites and have been visiting one and dropping gifts weekly for about a month. . . . Returned via the Curaray looking for possible landing beaches. Hopes not good . . . Guide us, Lord God."[1] That selection was written only three months before his death.

During that year Elisabeth and I shared many breakfasts and dinners. I'm sure she was somewhat amused by my Southern accent, gushy personality, and my insistence that seminary men and women could actually be "just friends." Really.

From Elisabeth I learned the proper way to eat an artichoke (my first!), how to clean grout in shower stalls with a toothbrush (I wasn't very good at it), and . . . the biblical response to suffering.

She never set out to teach me this, but you can't be around a godly person who is acquainted with suffering without somehow embracing Truth. Even her own college pastor had once said to her, "If your life is broken when given to Jesus, it may be because pieces will feed a multitude whereas a loaf would only satisfy a lad."

All I knew was that in 1977, *I* was one of the multitude being fed as a result of the broken pieces of her life.

One of the most transfiguring truths she willingly imparts to all who will receive it is that of our being called to *share* the sufferings of Christ. The apostle Peter wrote,

"Rejoice that you participate in the sufferings of Christ, so that you may be overjoyed when his glory is revealed" (1 Pet. 4:13). Elisabeth Elliot put it this way:

> It's up to God to change hearts. It's up to us to do the simple (not always easy), humble, sacrificial thing, and to faithfully leave the rest to God.
> In difficulties of all kinds I've been wonderfully helped by taking time to look at them in light of Christ Himself. Do you know the hymn, "Beneath the Cross of Jesus"? (If not, you'd find it a great comfort to learn by heart.) That is where we must take our stand. It was at the cross that Jesus dealt with all our sins, griefs, and sorrows. He calls us to give up all right to ourselves, take up the cross, and follow. This hard place in which you perhaps find yourself, so painful and bewildering, is the very place in which God is giving you the opportunity to look only to Him, to travail in prayer, and to learn long-suffering, gentleness, meekness—in short, to learn the depths of love that Christ Himself has poured out on all of us. . . . This form of suffering is your opportunity to learn to *leave with God what only God can do.*[2]

Back in my youth I was concerned that I had never really suffered, at least not compared to the dramatic suffering of many of God's people. Yet Elisabeth Elliot's own definition of suffering—"wanting what you don't have and having what you don't want"—makes it clear that we all are acquainted with suffering to some extent.

Amy Carmichael's poem "No Scar?" prompted me to pray Paul's prayer in Philippians 3:10: "I want to know Christ and the power of his resurrection and the fellowship of sharing in his sufferings . . . . "

No Scar?

Hast thou no scar?
    No hidden scar on foot, or side, or hand?
    I hear thee sung as mighty in the land,
    I hear them hail thy bright ascendant star,
    Hast thou no scar?
Hast thou no wound?
    Yet I was wounded by the archers, spent,
    Leaned Me against a tree to die; and rent
    By ravening beasts that compassed Me, I swooned:
    Hast thou no wound?
No wound? No scar?
    Yet, as the Master shall the servant be,
    And pierced are the feet that follow Me;
    But thine are whole: Can he have followed far
    Who has nor wound nor scar?[3]

Well, God answered my prayers. I now have scars. I now have wounds. Be careful what you pray for!

Most of our scars are hidden, but Dave Roever has scars for everyone to see! He says, "I've gone through hell, and I'm still coming back. God has taken a tragedy and turned it into his triumph." There is even a documentary film about his life entitled *Scars That Heal.*

When Dave was eighteen years old and in the Navy, he was burned over 40 percent of his body from a phosphorous hand grenade. Nearly half of his face and chest were gone. As a burn victim, Roever spent fourteen months recovering in the hospital. After viewing himself in the mirror, he decided he didn't want to live and pulled a tube from his body. But he pulled the wrong one.

"I'm glad," he says. "I would have missed twenty-three years of my life."

Only months before leaving for Vietnam, he had married his childhood sweetheart, Brenda. When she arrived at the hospital, she walked over to Dave, who was identifiable only by his hospital chart, and said, "I want you to know I really love you. Welcome home, Davey."

Shortly after his release from the hospital Roever tried to bargain with God to get his scars removed. Then, committing his life to God, he said, "With or without these scars, Your grace is sufficient."

The scarred tissue on Roever's face and hands is evidence of the healing. Roever explains, "No one wants scars, but if having them is the alternative to death, then bring them on. If there is no healing spiritually, then there is no healing."[4]

Oswald Chambers, in *My Utmost for His Highest*, says that "No normal, healthy saint ever chooses suffering; he simply chooses God's will, just as Jesus did, whether it means suffering or not." When you and I pray that God's will be done in our lives, we must mean it—no matter what it costs us—for truly He will take us at our word."[5]

Too many people falsely assume that life should be void of fear, loneliness, confusion, and doubt. But Henri Nouwen put great value on that which makes us "wounded healers." He wrote, "Our sufferings can only be dealt with creatively when they are understood as wounds integral to our human condition. Therefore ministry is a very comforting service. It does not allow people to live with illusions of immortality and wholeness. It keeps reminding others that they are mortal and broken, but also that with the recognition of this condition, liberation starts."[6]

Paul began his second letter to the Corinthians with the same thought: "Praise be to the God and Father of our Lord Jesus Christ, the Father of compassion and the God of all comfort, who comforts us in all our troubles, so that we can comfort those in any trouble with the comfort we ourselves have received from God. For just as the sufferings of Christ flow over into our lives, so also through Christ our comfort overflows" (2 Cor. 1:3–5).

This is so true—nothing is wasted with God! Recently I was traveling out of state and had the opportunity to spend the night with an old friend from seminary days. Although we had not seen each other in the fifteen years since I was in her wedding, we had kept in touch through Christmas cards and the occasional letter. Though I loved this friend dearly, I had long ago felt envious of her. She always seemed to be prettier, smarter, and more talented than me. I knew from her Christmas picture that she was still thin and beautiful with four tow-headed kids. I don't know what she was thinking about me as she anticipated our reunion, but I was a bit nervous.

What I do know is that within two minutes of our hug, the years melted away. Here we were, two forty-something women sitting at the kitchen table licking the chocolate icing off the spatula as though we had just made a cake in the dorm kitchen. Almost immediately she shared with me some terribly deep waters her family was now passing through—similar waters to those which had almost drowned me in years past. And because of my own suffering, I was able to offer her the comfort which I had received from God.

Later she told me she was surprised she had revealed so much. "I wasn't even planning to tell you about this. I thought we could just have a nice evening catch-up conversation and then I'd take you to the airport in the morning." But something in me must have communicated to her that it was okay to reveal wounds. I'd like to think it was grace.

There is no value in suffering, per se, but there can be great value in how we respond to it. Will we become bitter or better? British evangelist David Watson once observed, "Suffering can often produce great depths of character,

mature understanding, warm compassion and rich spiritu-
ality. . . . it can make us more like Christ."[7]

The sparkling radiance of a diamond is caused when a
lump of coal is subjected to extreme pressure and heat over
a long period of time. A beautiful pearl emerges when an
oyster has to cover an irritating object with layer upon layer
of smooth mother-of-pearl lining excreted from its own
body. Watson makes the connection: "When we suffer in
various ways, God is able to use all the pressures and
irritations to reveal something of His radiance and beauty
in our lives."[8]

I allow the process of suffering to transform me into
the image of Christ only when I'm willing to let go of who
I think I *ought* to be and become who God wants me to be.
Perhaps you, as I, always desired to be a beautiful Ming
vase in God's service when in actuality He has chosen to
channel His love through us as chipped clay pots. He
doesn't want the loaf of bread to feed a lad, but the broken
pieces to feed a multitude.

On the wall of Elisabeth Elliot's study which overlooks
the majestic New England coastline is a small plaque with
these words by Ugo Bassi:

Measure thy life by loss, not by gain.
Not by the wine drunk, but by the wine poured out.
For love's strength standeth in sacrifice.
And He that suffereth most has most to give.

One psychologist says that a few joyful folk know that
what their souls yearn for is coming. Larry Crabb explains,
"They enjoy the good things available now, tolerating with
cheerful grace the imperfections. These mature saints
speak of a deep longing for what is not yet theirs, a deep
longing that sometimes becomes an intense ache of the
soul. Honest Christians hurt. Mature honest Christians
understand groaning but surround their hurt with the joy

of service and anticipation."⁹ Now that's the kind of old woman I want to be!

A counselor once said to me, "Cindy, camp out in the pain." But we don't want to hear these things when we hurt. We want *out*. We are like the little boy who had a cocoon. Impatient to release the butterfly, he took some scissors and cut it open, thus destroying the eventual beauty. We'd like to bypass the process, but if we did, we'd miss the hidden beauty.

One of my favorite stories is about a couple: whenever one of them started to complain about the tedious process of a chore, the other would reprimand with the words "Long walk." Immediately there would be a change in attitude. One day a friend asked them what these secret code words between them meant.

It seems that years before, the couple was in Africa and received from one of the villagers a beautiful polished shell—a kind which could only be found on a faraway beach. As the wife exclaimed her joy and gratitude at such a lovely gift, the African merely said, "Long walk."

Puzzled, the lady said, "Pardon?"

He then explained, "Long walk part of gift."

And so it is with us. As much as we'd like to push the "fast forward" button to the end results, it is the lessons learned during the suffering which are so valuable.

In the waning days of 1976, I was privileged to hear firsthand of how Christ meets us in the middle of our sufferings. Dr. Helen Roseveare, a medical missionary to Zaire, addressed 17,000 students at InterVarsity's triennial missions convention in Urbana, Illinois. At the ripe old age of twenty-three I ended up being one of the chaperones for a busload of North Carolina college students. (When God wants you to hear a special message, He'll use any means He needs to get you there!)

Dr. Roseveare had us all spellbound as she described the Mau Mau rebellion in the Belgian Congo in October 1964. She explained how she was captured, savagely beaten, and raped. Recalling those events, she said she knew someone back home must have been praying for her because she was past praying in the middle of it all. Suddenly she had known that God was there in all His majesty and power—surrounding her with his love and whispering, "Twenty years ago you asked me for the privilege of being a missionary. This is it. Don't you want it?"

Looking at the thousands of bright, eager baby boomers who were hanging on every word, Roseveare drove her point home:

> Fantastic. The privilege of being identified with our Savior. As I was driven down the short corridor of my home, it was as though He clearly said to me, "These are not your sufferings. They are not beating you. These are my sufferings. All I ask of you is the loan of your body." An enormous relief swept through me: One word became unbelievably clear. That word was *privilege.* He did not take away the pain or cruelty or humiliation. No, it was all there, but now it was altogether different. It was with Him, for Him, in Him. He was actually offering me the inestimable privilege of sharing in some little way in the fellowship of His suffering.
>
> In the weeks of imprisonment that followed and in the subsequent years of continual service, I have looked back and tried to "count the cost," but I find it all swallowed up in privilege.[10]

Is God really there for those who grieve? Will He truly bestow on them "beauty instead of ashes, the oil of gladness instead of mourning, and a garment of praise instead of a spirit of despair" (Isa. 61:3)? Yes. A thousand times yes.

Of course, sometimes our view of the time to provide the beauty for ashes doesn't line up with God's timing, and we suffer even more as we fight against His purposes.

When our son, Timothy, was seven years old he loved playing G. I. Joe. One day as Tim and I were going through the checkout counter at the corner drug store, he thrust a G. I. Joe figure onto the counter and asked if I would buy it for him.

I knew that his birthday was in a few days and that his daddy and I had purchased the super duper G. I. Joe tank. In fact, it was wrapped and hiding in my closet at that very moment. But, of course, Tim didn't know that. I told him that we couldn't buy the action figure just now.

"You never say yes to anything!" he erupted.

I felt bad, but I held my ground. I knew that I was saying no to this small G. I. Joe figure because in a few short days I had an even better present prepared for him.

How often I have done the same thing with God! When I pray for something and He says no, it's usually because He knows that He has something even better in store for me down the line.

When I visited Elisabeth Elliot recently, she reiterated to me that the *circumstances* of our pain are not to be our focus. She said, "Suffering can be a path to holiness only for those open to the training—not by arguing with the Lord about what we did or did not do to deserve this, but by praying, 'Lord, show me what you have for me in this.' Not 'after this' or 'instead of this' but '*in* this.'"

Don't wait until the lessons are fully learned, but seek to know and serve Him in the middle of the pain. Amy Carmichael's poem serves as a prayer:

Before the winds that blow do cease,
    Teach me to dwell within Thy calm.

Before the pain has passed in peace,
    Give me, my God, to sing a psalm.
Let me not lose the chance to prove
    The fullness of enabling love.
O Love of God, do this for me,
    Maintain a constant victory.[11]

One week from today I am scheduled to travel to Boston to speak to a gathering of women on the topic of "Finding Hope among the Ruins." If this group is like most, there will be every form of suffering imaginable (and a few I've never imagined) represented in that room. Many of the conferees will feel as though they have failed God so miserably that He couldn't possibly want them on His team. They will be almost desperate for a word of hope, for the promise that they are not damaged goods, useless for God's kingdom. They need what we all need—a strong word of hope to help them along in rebuilding their lives.

What will I say? Well, I'll teach from Isaiah 61, the passage about all God wants to give us—beauty for ashes, gladness for mourning, and praise for despair. But I'll also share with them Patricia St. John's marvelous poem, "The Alchemist," in which she portrays a Christ who cements our sad experience with His grace in order to build a stronger temple of His own.

Build away, Lord, build away.

◆

Amazing Applications

1. God uses our sufferings to conform us to His likeness. Think of someone who has been used to encourage you in your own faith journey. Did that person experience a special trial or challenge in life? Read and underline in your Bible 2 Corinthians 1:3–7. Pray that God might redeem your suffering by using you to comfort others.

2. Are you surprised that one of the privileges of being a believer in Christ is that of suffering for His Name's sake? Do you know that God's grace will be sufficient in our sufferings? Look up these passages for "proof." Philippians 1:29–30; Romans 5:3–5; James 1:2–4; and 1 Peter 1:6–7.

3. Dave Roever said that the alternative to healing is death. If you have suffered, you can be healed. Sure, the scars will remain (whether visible, like Dave's, or invisible), but you can once again be a whole person. What scars do you have? Pray now that God would touch you with His healing hand. Know also that sometimes His healing of the body is perfected only in heaven. We don't have to understand why some are physically healed and some are not on this earth. But Christ says that *all* can be healed from emotional and spiritual wounds.

4. Has your suffering made you bitter? If so, then you are suffering all the more due to your own stubbornness! You cannot regain the "lost years" when you perhaps wallowed in your bitterness. But you can take charge of the rest of your life. Seek out others to encourage and healing will come.

◆

Grace Memory Verse
And the God of all *grace*,
who called you to his eternal glory in Christ,
after you have suffered a little while,
will himself restore you
and make you strong, firm and steadfast.
—1 Peter 5:10—
◆

CHAPTER TWELVE

Acclaimed as Victors

ac·'claimed *vb:* declared by loud eager applause

*F*or some it was a field of dreams. For me it was a field of shame. I recently returned to Jerger Elementary School in Thomasville, Georgia, only to discover that in thirty-five years the once formidable playing field had shrunk!

At seven years old I already dreaded recess. That's when the captains would alternately choose up for softball or kickball teams. Chubby and uncoordinated, I was always the last one chosen. I learned early in life what an athletic winner was like. And it was not me.

Perhaps that's when I started trying harder—and never stopped. But I slowed down significantly when I discovered that through God's grace I had already been declared a winner!

Donald W. McCullough, in his book *Waking from the American Dream* used this analogy: "Grace means that in the middle of our struggle the referee blows the whistle and announces the end of the game. We are declared winners and sent to the showers. It's over for all the huffing, puffing piety to earn God's favor; it's finished for all the sweat-soaked straining to secure self-worth; it's the end of all the competitive scrambling to get ahead of others in the game. *Grace means that God is on our side and thus we are victors regardless of how well we have played the game.* We might as well head for the showers and the champagne celebration."[1]

What a surge of hope and adrenaline to know that because I have chosen to follow Christ I am a victor in the only game that really matters! Whether I run the race with speed or merely slow determination, I'm still the victor. Whether I keep my eyes on the goal or allow myself to become sidetracked, I'm still the victor. Whether I beat all world records in my quest for a godly and purposeful life or merely cross the finish line crawling on bloody knees, I am still the victor. It is, as Friedrich Nietzsche once said, "a long obedience in the same direction."

The Christian life is not a quiet escape to a garden where we can walk and talk to our Lord without interruption. Nor is it a fantasy trip to a heavenly city where we compare our blue ribbons and gold medals to others who have also made it to the winner's circle. It is, as Eugene Peterson says, "going to God."

> In going to God Christians travel the same ground that everyone else walks on, breathe the same air, drink the same water, shop in the same stores, read the same newspapers, are citizens under the same governments, pay the same prices for groceries and gasoline, fear the same dangers, are subject to the same pressures, get the same distresses, are buried in the same ground.
>
> The difference is that each step we walk, each breath we breathe, we know we are preserved by

God, we know we are accompanied by God, we know we are ruled by God; and therefore no matter what doubts we endure or what accidents we experience, the Lord will preserve us from evil, He will keep our life.[2]

Today I stand on a different field. Actually, it's not really a field but the massive tennis courts of Yale University. I think of the many distinguished professionals who have competed here in international events such as the Volvo Tournament.

In two short months my own son, Justin, will join seven thousand other athletes from 140 countries to compete in the Special Olympics World Games. He will represent the USA in men's singles and mixed doubles competition. This young man of mine who, twenty short years ago, was born mentally retarded—who struggled for years to learn to write his name, to tie his shoes finally at age ten, to read at a first-grade level, count money, dial a telephone, and open a catfood can without cutting himself. At times, as a young child, Justin would get so frustrated at his own inability to communicate or accomplish simple tasks that his younger brother and sister could easily do, that he would scream and act out uncontrollably.

Today he is a handsome young man who easily carries on a conversation with adults, earns "employee of the week" at his job, faithfully does his daily devotions, and even leads the games at our church's Vacation Bible School. He is one of my most favorite people to be around, and we often go on "dates."

As I look at Justin, I marvel at the grace of God which has so beautifully transformed and carried him these past years. He has endured ridicule (shouts of "retardo" on the school bus) and deep disappointments (not being able to drive like other teens), and overcome significant challenges (from needing physical therapy to now being an outstanding athlete in six different sports). Just this week he adroitly handled a fifty-minute television interview with the CBS anchor, Al Terzi at WFSB.

It's no wonder I am filled with righteous anger at those people who advocate choosing which babies have the right to enter this world and which babies are expendable! The world has spent millions of dollars advocating values that clearly say people like Justin are not winners. Are they ever wrong! I have spent the last twelve years as his number one cheerleader and prayer warrior.

I don't know whether my son will come home this summer with a gold medal or not. It really doesn't matter. What I do know is that *he is already a winner.* One week after the world games, he leaves on a mission trip to Kentucky to repair homes for the poor. Then he's back at his annual summer job at Deerfoot Lodge, a Christian boys camp in the New York Adirondacks.*

The Special Olympics, founded in 1968 by Eunice Kennedy Shriver, is an organization in which everyone wins. If you haven't experienced the Special Olympics, I invite you to attend your local competition. Actually, I dare you to sign up as a volunteer. (This summer's World Games will require more than 45,000 volunteers.) One simply cannot watch the wheelchair track events or the ice-skating, swimming, bowling, and soccer without seeing in all this interplay a perfect picture of God's grace.

You see, the competition is set up in such a way that everyone wins. Preparing to compete, learning teamwork, training in health and nutrition, traveling independently,

---

*Author's note: At the 1995 Special Olympics World Games, Justin McDowell won the gold medal for men's singles tennis and a second gold medal for mixed doubles tennis with his partner, Grace Knechtle.

and wearing a uniform are just as important for the Special Olympics athletes as the awards ceremony. *How* we live each day of our lives is as important as knowing we will be in heaven one day with Jesus Christ.

On my car (the family taxi) I have a small decal with lupines on it—the beautiful tall purple flowers that grow in Maine and elsewhere. They are there for a purpose—to remind me of Miss Rumphius. Do you know *Miss Rumphius?* Perhaps you should.

Alice Rumphius is the creation of author and artist Barbara Cooney who still lives in Damariscotta, Maine. When Alice was a little girl, she listened to her grandfather tell stories of his life. When he had finished, Alice would say, "When I grow up, I too will go to faraway places, and when I grow old, I too will live beside the sea."

But her grandfather told her that there was a third thing she must also do. "You must do something to make the world more beautiful."

But Alice didn't know what that could be.

Miss Alice Rumphius grew up, became a librarian, and traveled to many exotic places. She retired in a little cottage by the sea and one spring was quite ill. Looking out her window she noticed lupines in the faraway fields and had an idea.

By the next spring she was feeling better and ordered five bushels of lupine seed. All that summer Miss Rumphius wandered over the countryside flinging handfuls of lupine seed. People sometimes called her "that crazy old lady."

But the next spring there were lupines everywhere. Fields and hillsides were covered with blue and purple and rose-colored flowers. Miss Rumphius had done the third, most difficult thing of all!

The book ends with a very elderly Miss Rumphius (now lovingly called "the Lupine Lady") sitting in her parlor telling stories to a circle of children. Her grandniece tells her that when she grows up, she, too, will go to faraway places and come home to live by the sea.

"That is all very well," says her great-aunt Alice, "but there is a third thing you must do. You must do something to make the world more beautiful."[3]

That's why I keep the lupine decal on my car. It reminds me of the most important thing of all—to leave behind something beautiful. As someone once said, "We should all plant a few trees we'll never sit under."

But sometimes we get discouraged along the way. *Pilgrim's Progress*, written by John Bunyan in 1675 while he was imprisoned in the Bedford Jail, reveals very clearly the place of grace in our journey of faith. As I mentioned before, it is the allegory of a pilgrim named Christian who travels from the City of Destruction to the Holy City, encountering all sorts of trials along the way.

At one point in the story, Interpreter takes Christian to a place where a fire is burning against a wall. There is a man standing next to it, constantly throwing buckets of water on it to quench the flames. Yet the fire burns hotter and hotter. Christian is confused and asks the meaning of all this.

Interpreter answers, "The fire is the work of grace in the heart and he who casts water upon it, trying to extinguish it, is the Devil. But let me show you why the fire continues to burn higher and hotter."

So he took Christian around to the backside of the wall to show him another man who kept pouring oil into the fire.

"This is Christ who continually, with the oil of His grace, maintains the work already begun in the heart. . . . And you saw the man standing behind the wall to maintain the fire, teaching you that it is hard for the tempted to see how his work of grace is maintained in the soul."[4]

Has your zeal for God ever dwindled to nothing more than a smoldering wick? Has the Enemy come close to literally putting a wet blanket on all your hopes and dreams? Don't worry. For those who have Christ, He *continues* to do a good work in you. And His oil of grace is an endless supply.

Even such spiritual giants as A. W. Tozer occasionally had difficulty surrendering all to follow Christ, as his prayer reflects:

> Father, I want to know Thee, but my coward heart fears to give up its toys. I cannot part with them without inward bleeding and I do not try to hide from Thee the terror of the parting. I come trembling, but I do come. Please root from my heart all those things which I have cherished for so long and which have become a very part of my living self so that Thou mayest enter and dwell there without a rival. . . . then Thou shalt make the place of Thy feet glorious. Then shall my heart have no need of the sun to shine in it, for Thyself will be the light of it. AMEN.[5]

Perhaps you've never wholly surrendered your heart and soul to the One who created you, loves you with an everlasting love, and has called you His child. Why live another moment in uncertainty? Don't you want to be the victor when the last trumpet sounds? If you are living with some uncertainty in your spiritual walk, you can know today that you too will one day be present with God at the Feast by sharing the following prayer with God in your own words:

> Heavenly Father,
> I am really a selfish person. I have wanted my own way—not Yours. I have often been jealous,

proud and rebellious. You are my Creator, but I have acted as though I was lord of all. I have not been thankful to You. I have not listened to Your Word the Bible and have not loved Your Son Jesus. But now I see that all my sin is against You. I now repent of this evil attitude. I turn from all my sins and trust that Jesus shed His precious blood to cleanse me from all my guilt. I now receive Him as my Savior and the Lord of my life. Amen.

I, _____, turn from my sins and take Christ as my Lord and Savior. By His help I promise to obey Him in every part of my life.

Date _____.[6]

Welcome to the family! You are a son or daughter of the King! Now live like it!

Earlier in this book I mentioned Dave Dravecky. Because he prayed a prayer such as that one day, victory came to have a whole new meaning for him. After his cancer-riddled pitching arm was amputated, he was interviewed on the *Good Morning, America* television show. Interviewer Charlie Gibson began by asking him, "Where does someone find the grace to cope with a tragic irony like that?"

Dave Dravecky knew the answer.

In the hands of a heavenly Father. He gives us the grace to face life's uncertainties, its disappointments, and its tragedies.

There's a story in *The Hiding Place* where the young Corrie ten Boom sees a baby who has died and curiously touches its face. The feel of the cold and lifeless skin startles her. Suddenly she realizes that if death could take this little baby, no one was safe, not even the loved ones in her family. The thought terrified her and caused her to burst into

tears. This is how Corrie's father helps her understand the grace of God:
"Father sat down on the edge of the narrow bed.
'Corrie,' he began gently, 'when you and I go to Amsterdam—when do I give you your ticket?'
She sniffed a few times, considering this.
'Why, just before we get on the train.'
'Exactly. And our wise Father in heaven knows when we're going to need things, too. Don't run out ahead of Him, Corrie. When the time comes that some of us will have to die, you will look into your heart and find the strength you need—just in time."
I'm not getting through the loss of my arm because I am a great coper. I'm getting through it because I have a Father in heaven who is a great giver. *He* is where I find the grace. At the time I need strength, he puts it in my heart or provides it through someone who is close to me, whether that's a family doctor or simply a friend. I don't earn it. I don't deserve it. I don't bring it about. It's a gift. And that is how I am able to cope with the "tragic irony" of losing my arm.[7]

Our ultimate victory will be to join Him in heaven one day. That's a promise. Henry, a Ugandan Christian whose face was blown away in a guerrilla ambush during the reign of Idi Amin, was flown to Canada by World Vision for reconstructive surgery. As the innovative British preacher David Watson was dying from cancer, he wrote in his book *Fear No Evil* about meeting Henry. David flinched to see Henry's bandaged face but noticed that his eyes were quite lively. Since the man was unable to speak he wrote this note to David: "God never promises us an easy time. Just *a safe arrival.*"[8] That is the hope of victory that all we in Christ can know.

Like you, I have occasionally wondered about the circumstances of my own "safe arrival." Will I be young? old? die naturally? die violently? Will I be *ready?* Well, it certainly is a waste of time to think on these things. Like Corrie, I don't really need to know ahead of time—I just need to know that God is sovereign and His timing is perfect.

But I do think about heaven, perhaps because I've now reached "middle-age" and have quite a few loved ones there already. One description returns to mind. It is from C. S. Lewis' *Chronicles of Narnia* which I first read as a child. In the seventh book, *The Last Battle,* Peter, Edmund, and Lucy go farther up and farther in, where they see Aslan the Lion who has been the Christ figure throughout the series. Now he is leaping down the mountain to greet them:

> "There was a real railway accident; your father and mother and all of you are—as you used to call it in the Shadowlands—dead. The term is over: the holidays have begun. The dream is ended: this is the morning!"
>
> And as He spoke He no longer looked to them like a lion; but the things that began to happen after that were so great and beautiful that I cannot write them. And for us this is the end of all the stories, and we can most truly say that they all lived happily ever after. But for them it was only the beginning of the real Story. All their life in this world and all their adventures in Narnia had only been the cover and the title page: now at last they were beginning Chapter One of the Great Story which no one on earth has read: which goes on forever: in which every chapter is better than the one before.[9]

Since I have dedicated this book to my husband and children, I would like to close with the benediction I offer them—and all of us—on this journey of grace:

"Now may the radical justice of God the Father, the liberating forgiveness of God the Son, and the revolutionary transforming presence of God the Holy Spirit so blow through your lives that you may go forth into this broken world and fight the Lamb's War knowing that the Risen King has already won the Victory over injustice, violence and death.
Hallelujah! AMEN."[10]

◆

Amazing Applications

1. None of us can change what has happened in the past. But we can, through God's grace, live in such a way that we *finish well*. One seminary homework assignment that gave me great perspective was to write my own obituary. That's right. Why don't you try it? Perhaps you will see areas that have been lacking in your life. Ask God to help you, *from now on*, live so you may truly finish well.

2. Perhaps you prayed that prayer surrendering your whole life to the Lordship of Jesus Christ. What now? You have begun a marvelous journey which gets even better as you exercise some basic spiritual disciplines:

◆ Pray constantly—Prayer is talking to Jesus. Be sure to include praise, thanksgiving, confession of sins, requests for help, and petitions for others to come to know Him.

◆ Read your Bible—Be sure you put God's Word into your heart every day. If you don't know where to begin, start with the Gospel of John. There you will meet Jesus and learn to claim His promises for your life.

♦ Worship with others—Few can live the Christian life as a lone ranger! Meet with a church family where the Bible is taught and obeyed and Jesus Christ is Lord and Savior.

♦ Witness to others—That's right! Tell your friends what Christ has done for you, remembering that people can challenge our theology, but they can never dispute what God has done in our lives. Be tactful and back up your words by a transformation in your behavior. People will believe what you do, more than what you say.

♦ Reread this book in one year—With your new eyes of faith, you may be amazed at the new messages God has in store for you to receive.

3. Plan your funeral or memorial service. Pick Scripture and music which are a celebration of your new life in eternity. At Winston Churchill's funeral the military band played "Taps" as he had requested. But then they followed it with a rousing rendition of "Reveille," also at his prior request. Churchill knew that death was not only an end, but also a beginning.

4. At least twice in Scripture Paul used the imagery of victors in a race to describe our heavenly victory: "Run in such a way as to get the prize. Everyone who competes in the games goes into strict training. They do it to get a crown that will not last; but we do it to get a crown that will last forever" (1 Cor. 9:24–25) and "I press on to take hold of that for which Christ Jesus took hold of me. Brothers, I do not consider myself yet to have taken hold of it. But one thing I do: Forgetting what is behind and straining toward what is ahead, I press on toward the goal to win the prize for which God has called me heavenward in Christ Jesus" (Phil.

3:12–14). What must *you* do today in order to win the race tomorrow?

◆

Grace Memory Verse

But we see Jesus, who was made a little lower than the angels, now crowned with glory and honor

because he suffered death, so that by the *grace* of God he might taste death for everyone.

—Hebrews 2:9—

◆

Notes

Chapter 1. Amazed by Grace

1. Charles R. Swindoll, *The Grace Awakening* (Waco, Tex.: Word Publishing, 1990), 42–43.
2. Lewis Smedes, *How Can It Be All Right When Everything Is All Wrong?* (New York: Harper and Row Publishers, 1982), 9–10.
3. William Carey, quoted in Jerry Bridges, *The Disciplines of Grace* (Colorado Springs, Colo.: NavPress, 1994), 29–30.
4. Ibid., 30–31.
5. Walter Wangerin Jr., *Little Lamb, Who Made Thee?* (Grand Rapids, Mich.: Zondervan Publishers, 1993), 70–71.
6. Kay Arthur, *Lord, I Need Grace to Make It* (Sisters, Oreg.: Multnomah, 1989), 21.

7. David A. Seamands, *Freedom from the Performance Trap* (Wheaton, Ill.: Victor Books, 1988), 109–10.
8. James Montgomery Boice, *Amazing Grace* (Wheaton, Ill.: Tyndale House Publishers, 1993), 34.
9. Donald Gray Barnhouse, *Romans: Man's Ruin, Volume I* (Grand Rapids, Mich.: William B. Eerdmans, 1952), 72.
10. RoseMarie Miller, *From Fear to Freedom* (Wheaton, Ill.: Harold Shaw Publishers, 1994), 4–5.
11. Elisabeth Elliot, *Twelve Baskets of Crumbs* (Chappaqua, N. Y.: Christian Herald House, 1976), 65.

Chapter 2. Afflicted in Spirit

1. Judith Viorst, *Alexander and the Terrible, Horrible, No Good, Very Bad Day* (New York: Macmillan Publishing Company, 1972).
2. Ibid.
3. Archibald Hart, "Understanding Depression," *Focus on the Family Magazine* (March 1993): 5–6.
4. Frank B. Minirth, M.D., and Paul D. Meier, M.D., *Happiness Is a Choice* (Grand Rapids, Mich.: Baker Book House, 1978), 108.
5. David A. Seamands, *Freedom from the Performance Trap* (Wheaton, Ill.: Victor Books, 1988), 168.
6. Ibid., 169.
7. Kent and Barbara Hughes, *Liberating Ministry from the Success Syndrome* (Wheaton, Ill.: Tyndale House Publishers, 1988), 31.
8. Patsy Clairmont, "Under His Wings," *Focus on the Family Magazine* (January 1995): 6.
9. Ibid., 6.
10. Jane J. Struck, "Jan Dravecky's Comeback," *Today's Christian Woman* (January/February 1993): 23.

11. Christina Rossetti, "A Better Resurrection," *Eerdman's Book of Christian Poetry* (Grand Rapids, Mich.: William B. Eerdmans Publishing Co., 1981), 62.
12. Gail MacDonald, *A Step Farther and Higher* (Sisters,Oreg.: Questar Publishers, 1993), 182.
13. Paul Thigpen, "Monica," *Discipleship Journal* (November/December 1994): 51.
14. Clairmont, "Under His Wings," 6.

Chapter 3. Approved in Christ
1. Max Lucado, *He Still Moves Stones* (Waco, Tex.: Word Publishing, 1993), 59.
2. Barbra Goodyear Minar, *Unrealistic Expectations* (Wheaton, Ill.: Victor Books, 1990), 39.
3. Charles R. Swindoll, *Growing in Grace with Charles R. Swindoll Calendar* (Outreach Publications, Inc., 1993), selection from February 15.
4. Jeff Van Vonderan, *Families Where Grace Is in Place* (Minneapolis, Minn.: Bethany House, 1992), 15.
5. Brennan Manning, *Abba's Child* (Colorado Springs, Colo.: NavPress, 1994), 30.
6. Lucinda Secrest McDowell, "Elisabeth Elliot on Writing, Speaking and God's Gifts," *The Christian Writer* (April 1991): 4.
7. Ruth Senter, *Longing for Love* (Colorado Springs, Colo.: NavPress, 1991), 38, 41.
8. Kevin Miller, "Do You REALLY Believe God Loves You?" *Today's Christian Woman* (November/December 1993): 62–63.

Chapter 4. Astonished by Sin
1. Cynthia Heald, *Becoming a Woman of Excellence* (Colorado Springs, Colo.: NavPress, 1986), 92.
2. Brian Abel Ragen, "America," quoted in *Discipleship Journal* (January 29, 1994): 18.

3. Larry Crabb, *Men and Women* (Grand Rapids, Mich.: Zondervan Publishers, 1991), 75, 87.
4. Rebecca Manley Pippert, *Hope Has Its Reasons* (San Francisco, Calif.: Harper San Francisco, 1989), 106–7.
5. Joseph Bayly, *Out of My Mind: The Best of Joseph Bayly.*
6. Jerry Bridges, *The Disciplines of Grace* (Colorado Springs, Colo.: NavPress, 1994), 35.
7. Steve Brown, *Overcoming Setbacks* (Colorado Springs, Colo.: NavPress, 1992), 79.
8. Mike Yaconelli, as quoted in Brennan Manning, *Abba's Child* (Colorado Springs, Colo.: NavPress, 1994), 52.
9. Manning, 152.
10. Ibid. 161.

Chapter 5. Adopted by God

1. David V. Andersen, "When God Adopts," *Christianity Today* (July 19,1993): 36.
2. Ibid., 37.
3. Brian Chapell, *In the Grip of Grace* (Grand Rapids, Mich.: Baker Book House, 1992), 36.
4. Philip Yancey and Tim Stafford, "Notes," *The Student Bible* (Grand Rapids, Mich.: Zondervan Publishing House, 1986), 1050.
5. Notes from "Sonship Week" Bible Course, Jack and Rose Marie Miller, lecturers.
6. Ibid.
7. Steve Brown, *Overcoming Setbacks* (Colorado Springs, Colo.: NavPress, 1992), 28.
8. Brennan Manning, *Abba's Child* (Colorado Springs, Colo.: NavPress, 1994), 23.

Chapter 6. Assaulted by Doubt

1. Steve Brown, *Overcoming Setbacks* (Colorado Springs, Colo.: NavPress, 1992), 59.
2. David A. Seamands, *Healing for Damaged Emotions* (Wheaton, Ill.: Victor Books, 1981), 49.

3. Timothy Warner, "Satan Hates You and Has a Terrible Plan for Your Life," *Discipleship Journal* (May/June 1994): 28.
4. Tom White, "Is This Really Warfare?" *Discipleship Journal* (May/June 1994): 34.
5. Warren and Ruth Myers, "Weapons That Work," *Discipleship Journal* (May/June 1994): 39.
6. Ibid.
7. Lloyd Ogilvie, *A Future and a Hope* (Waco, Tex.: Word Publishing, 1988), 70.
8. Gordon MacDonald, "Caring for the Spiritually Wounded," *Discipleship Journal* (May/June 1994): 30.
9. Brown, 60–61.
10. Brian Chapell, *In the Grip of Grace* (Grand Rapids, Mich.: Baker Book House, 1992), 135.

Chapter 7. Assisted in Freedom
1. Carol Kent, "When You're Afraid of Things That Haven't Happened Yet," *Today's Christian Woman* (July/August 1994): 73.
2. Susan Jeffers, *Feel the Fear and Do It Anyway* (New York: Ballantine Books, 1987), 218–19.
3. Carol Kent, *Tame Your Fears* (Colorado Springs, Colo.: NavPress, 1993), 52.
4. Mary Wilken, "Unpredictable Winds, Constant Grace," *Decision* (March 1993): 32.
5. Charles R. Swindoll, *The Grace Awakening* (Waco, Tex.: Word Publishers, 1990), 109.
6. Lois M. Wieder, *A Pleasant Land—A Goodly Heritage* (Wethersfield, Conn.: First Church of Christ in Wethersfield, Publishers, 1986), 68–69.
7. Ibid., 53.
8. Ibid.
9. Brian Chapell, *In the Grip of Grace* (Grand Rapids, Mich.: Baker Book House, 1992), 125.

10. Charles Colson, "The Volunteer at Auschwitz," *Focus on the Family* (January 1993): 3–4. (Also published in Colson, *The Body* (Waco, Tex.: Word Publishers, 1992), 325–29.

11. David A. Seamands, *Freedom from the Performance Trap* (Wheaton, Ill.: Victor Books, 1988), 67.

Chapter 8. Attracted to Godliness

1. Jerry Bridges, "Godliness, Something More than Christian Character," *Discipleship Journal* 18 (1983): 22.

2. Jerry Bridges, *The Discipline of Grace* (Colorado Springs, Colo.: NavPress, 1994), 94.

3. Arnold Lobel, *Frog and Toad Together* (New York: Harper and Row Publishers, 1971), 18–29.

4. Hannah Whitall Smith, *The Christian's Secret of a Happy Life* (Grands Rapids, Mich.: Fleming H. Revell, 1952), 201.

5. Karen Burton Mains, *Friends and Strangers* (Waco, Tex.: Word Publishers, 1990), 8.

6. H. B. London Jr., and Neil B. Wiseman, *Pastors at Risk* (Wheaton, Ill.: Victor Books, 1993), interview with Jerry Bridges, 176–77.

7. Richard Foster, "Praying the Ordinary," *Discipleship Journal* 74 (March/April 1993): 37.

8. R. Kent Hughes, *Disciplines of Grace* (Wheaton, Ill.: Crossway Books, 1993), 195–96.

9. Rosemary Broughton, *Praying with Teresa of Avila* (St. Mary's Press, 1990), 49.

10. C. S. Lewis, *Mere Christianity* (Collins, 1942), 180.

Chapter 9. Assured of Love

1. Brennan Manning, *The Ragamuffin Gospel* (Sisters, Oreg.: Multnomah, 1990), 214.

2. Ibid., 86.

3. Brian Chapell, *In the Grip of Grace* (Grand Rapids, Mich.: Baker Book House, 1992), 131.
4. David A. Seamands, *Freedom from the Performance Trap* (Wheaton, Ill.: Victor Books, 1988), 116.
5. Margaret Wise Brown, *The Runaway Bunny* (New York: Harper and Row, 1942), last page.
6. Ruth Senter, *Longing for Love* (Colorado Springs, Colo.: NavPress, 1991), 27–28.
7. Elisabeth Elliot, *The Savage, My Kinsman Epilogue* (Ann Arbor, Mich.: Servant Books, 1981), 146.

Chapter 10. Anointed to Serve

1. Madeleine L'Engle, *Walking on Water* (Wheaton, Ill.: Harold Shaw Publishers, 1980), 61–62.
2. Amy Carmichael, *His Thoughts Said . . . His Father Said* (Ft. Washington, Penn.: Christian Literature Crusade, 1941), 32.
3. Steve Brown, *Overcoming Setbacks* (Colorado Springs, Colo.: NavPress, 1992), 237.
4. Henri J. M. Nouwen, *Gracias!* (New York: Harper and Row Publishers, 1983), 16.
5. Gail MacDonald, *A Step Farther and Higher* (Sisters, Oreg.: Questar Publishers, 1993), 177.
6. Joni Eareckson Tada, "Wanted: Sinners, Weaklings and Misfits," *Discipleship Journal* (November/December 1994): 66.
7. Henri J. M. Nouwen, *In the Name of Jesus* (Crossroads, 1991), 15–16.
8. Jill Briscoe, "What's Stopping You?" *Discipleship Journal* (January/February 1995): 68.
9. Oswald Chambers, *My Utmost for His Highest* (New York: Dodd, Mead and Company, 1935), 46.

Chapter 11. Acquainted with Suffering

1. Elisabeth Elliot, *Journals of Jim Elliot* (Grand Rapids, Mich.: Fleming H. Revell Co., 1978), 469–71.

2. Elisabeth Elliot, *The Elisabeth Elliot Newsletter* (Ann Arbor, Mich.: Servant Publications), 2.
3. Amy Carmichael, *Toward Jerusalem* (Ft. Washington, Penn.: Christian Literature Crusade, 1936), 85, used by permission.
4. W. Terry Whalin, "Scars That Heal—The Dave Roever Story," *Decision* (November 1993): 25.
5. Oswald Chambers, *My Utmost for His Highest* (New York: Dodd, Mead and Company, 1935), 223.
6. Henri J. M. Nouwen, *The Wounded Healer* (New York: Doubleday, 1972), 95.
7. David Watson, *Fear No Evil* (Wheaton, Ill.: Harold Shaw Publishers, 1984), 135.
8. Ibid.
9. Larry Crabb, *Men and Women* (Grand Rapids, Mich.: Zondervan Publishers, 1991), 42–43.
10. Helen Roseveare, "The Cost of Declaring His Glory," in *Declare His Glory Among the Nations* (Downers Grove, Ill.: InterVarsity Press, 1976), 210.
11. Amy Carmichael, *Rose from Brier* (Ft. Washington, Penn.: Christian Literature Crusade, 1933), 12, used by permission.

Chapter 12. Acclaimed as Victors
1. Donald W. McCullough, *Waking from the American Dream* (Downers Grove, Ill.: InterVarsity Press, 1988), 116.
2. Eugene Peterson, *A Long Obedience in the Same Direction* (Downers Grove, Ill.: InterVarsity Press, 1980), 40–41.
3. Barbara Cooney, *Miss Rumphius* (New York: Puffin Books, 1982), no page numbers.
4. John Bunyan, with notes by Warren Wiersbe, *The New Pilgrim's Progress* (Grand Rapids, Mich.: Discovery House Publishers, 1989), 42–43.

5. A.W. Tozer, quoted in *Virtue* (May/June 1992): 9.
6. Jack Miller, "Have You Ever Wanted a NEW LIFE?" tract.
7. Dave and Jan Dravecky, *When You Can't Come Back* (Grand Rapids, Mich.: Zondervan Publishing House, 1992), 181–182.
8. David Watson, *Fear No Evil* (Wheaton, Ill.: Harold Shaw Publishers, 1984), 141.
9. C. S. Lewis, *The Last Battle* (New York: Penguin Books, 1956), 165.
10. Ronald Sider, *Christ and Violence* (Scottsdale, Penn.: Herald Press, 1979), 101.

◆

About the Author

Lucinda Secrest McDowell, M.T.S., is a dynamic speaker and author from the Hartford, Connecticut, area. She currently serves as director of Caring Ministries at First Church of Christ Congregational in Wethersfield, a congregation that was "gathered" in 1635. She is a graduate of Gordon-Conwell Theological Seminary and Furman University and has studied at Wheaton Graduate School of Communication.

In addition to *Amazed by Grace*, Cindy is the editor of *Woman's Spiritual Passages* (Harold Shaw, 1996) and contributed to *The Strength of a Woman* (Broadman & Holman Publishers, 1993), *Shaped by God's Love* (Grason, 1990) and *Stepping Out—A Guide to Short-Term Missions* (YWAM Publishing, 1992). She has also published articles in more than fifty different magazines and, in 1993, was named "Writer of the Year" at the annual Mount Hermon Christian Writers Conference in California.

Cindy is married to the Reverend Michael McDowell and is the mother of two sons and two daughters.

She would love to hear from you. Please write her at:

Encouraging Words!
P.O. Box 290707
Wethersfield, CT 06129–0707

◆